Sweet Sorrows

Selected Poems of Sheikh Farideddin Attar Neyshaboori

Renditions by Vraje Abramian

HOHM PRESS
Chino Valley, Arizona

Cover Design: Adi Zuccarello
Cover Art: "Barbad Playing Music" by Khamsa of Nizami, in *Persian Painting: Five Royal Safavid Manuscripts of the 16th Century* by Stuart Cory Welch. (New York: George Braziller, Inc., 1976, p. 87.) Used with permission.

Interior Design and Layout: Kubera Book Design, Prescott, Arizona

Library of Congress Cataloging in Publication Data:

'Attar, Farid al-Din, d. ca. 1230
[Poems. Selections. English]
Sweet sorrows : selected poems of Sheikh Farideddin Attar Neyshaboori / Renditions by Vraje Abramian.
pages cm
Includes bibliographical references.
ISBN 978-1-935387-42-8 (trade pbk. : alk. paper)
I. Abramian, Vraje. II. Title.
PK6451.F4S913 2013
891'.5511--dc23

2013004589

Hohm Press
P.O. Box 4410
Chino Valley, AZ 86323
800-381-2700
http://www.hohmpress.com

Glory is You
whose praise,
though summons me to life
and loosens my tongue,
refuses to be uttered.

—Attar, *Divan*[1]

Other than the sweet sorrow of missing the Beloved
nothing lasts in either world.
If your share from here and hereafter
is a drop of this longing, rejoice,
for no better cure exists
for all the ills in all the worlds.

—Attar, *Divan*[2]

The Self is not known through the study of the scriptures, nor through subtlety of the intellect, nor through much learning. But by him who longs for him is he known. Verily unto him does the Self reveal his true being.

—Upanishads[3]

Humbly dedicated to Huzur
and to Baba-Ji

A long time past,
the Celestial Emperor shut his gate tight,
but today, in human guise,
He has appeared at the door to favor us.

—Rumi, *Divan of Shams*[4]

ACKNOWLEDGEMENTS

I am indebted to my wife Elizabeth Ruth for her patience and help in various stages of the preparation of the manuscript and to Regina Sara Ryan, editor, Hohm Press, for her masterful editing of the manuscript.

With these words, inadequate as they are, I would like to express my gratitude to the late Sohrab Alavinia, a Gonabady Nematollahi, in whose presence our conversation always seemed to move towards Attar, and who recited Attar's poems with that contagious delight reserved for those who share the Sheikh's longing.

He was a living product of a Tradition which throughout its history has produced men and women who temper a world-class intellect with that profound integrity and modesty that spirit alone knoweth, and who live lives of childlike joy in this "valley of tears," " . . . in the shadow of death."

Though it is impossible to grow up in Iran and not to know about Attar, it was only after I had spent some time with Sohrab that I began to appreciate the depths to which Sheikh Attar had plumbed and what his works have meant to practitioners since.

Sweet Sorrows was inspired by Sohrab's fiery love of Attar. I contracted this love, according to my capacity, while in Sohrab's company in Cambridge, Massachusetts, where he was an exchange professor from Tehran University. Our sojourn together, alas too fleeting and too short, was to lead to pastures more fragrant than I was yet able to realize. May his road Home be drenched in light.

CONTENTS

PREFACE

It would be no exaggeration to say that poetry is part of one's daily diet in Iran, and in cultures intimately associated with the Iranian civilization. Zoroaster is considered the first Iranian poet.[1] Post-Islamic Sufi poetry in Iran has a history that stretches beyond one thousand years. Through Rumi, and later Hafez, Persian reaches its dizzying heights and becomes a language of the caliber to be found in *Divan-e Shams-e Tabriz*, *Masnavi Manavee*, and the *Divan of Hafez*; a language extraordinarily well-equipped to express metaphysical intricacies and to thrive as the language of the spirit.[2]

Recitation of mystics' poems, with or without instrumental accompaniment, has for over a thousand years been a practice among various Sufi brotherhoods in their gatherings. As such, these words serve as portals into domains where human consciousness embarks on journeys beyond the realm of words.

> *Two thousand times a breath*
> *you would recite this qhazal*
> *if, beyond the boundaries of facts,*
> *you were able to trace its reach.*
>
> —Rumi[3]

To imagine that such an affair might be translatable is rather naive. Dr. Mohammad-Reza Shafie Kadkani—after mentioning

---

1 Jackson, A.V. Williams. *Early Persian Poetry*, Longwood Press Ltd., 1999, p. 115.

2 The fact that Persian is grammatically gender-free makes it possible to speak of love in a spiritual context without any danger of mistaking it for anything with carnal or sexual implications. It also preempts sexism as far as use of pronouns is concerned.

3 *Divan-e Shams Tabriz*, p. 1048, no. 2830. Personal translation by Vraje Abramian.

Jahez (d-976), the first in Iranian history to write on the impossibility of translating poetry: "Poetry becomes unintended prose and is lost in translation . . ."; and Seamus Heaney (b-1939): "Poets belong to the language, not to the world"; as well as Robert Frost (d-1963): "Poetry is what is lost in translation . . ."—continues to say that it is the translator's responsibility to propose appropriate equivalents while attempting literary translation.[4] Dr. Mojtaba Minavi (d-1976) also regards literary translation impossible: "Words are symbols whose secrets are decodable only by the speakers of that (same) language . . ."[5] "Thus the art of translation will always have to cope with the reality of untranslatability from one language to another," says Hugo Friedrich.[6]

Not a very promising start to any "translation" endeavor.

What remains then is the possibility that one may strive to render the content—the message—into the target language recreating it in a form which, while flowing naturally (in English), invites the reader's imagination in the direction the author intends (i.e., the translator's understanding thereof!). Here, to the extent one remains faithful to the unique flavor and style in the original version, the poet's voice stands a chance to be heard above that of the translator's.

In this collection, a number of Sheikh Attar's works from "Asrar-nameh" (AN), *The Book of Mysteries, the Divan of Attar* (DIV), "Elahee-nameh" (EN), *The Book of The Beloved*, "Mokhtar-nameh" (MKN), *The Book of the Sovereign*, "Moseebat-nameh" (MN), *The Book of Travails* and "Tazkirat-al Oliya" (TZK), and *Biography of the Saints* were selected. These pieces are numbered

---

4 *Bukhara Literary Magazine*, vol. 4, no. 80, pp. 82-88. Personal translation by Vraje Abramian.

5 Ibid., pp. 521-523.

6 Friedrich, Hugo. "On The Art of Translation," in *Theories of Translation*, (Ed. Rainer Shulte and John Biguene), Chicago: The Univ. of Chicago Press, 1992, p. 11.

in the sequence they appear in the collection; source, page and line numbers are given in the endnotes.

Attar's poetry reveals our Sheikh's personal witness to the sanctity and oneness of all life, and to his unflinching faith in human potential and his/her ultimate worth. He never tires of pointing out to the individual that in the midst of the uncertainty and the baffling apparent chaos of (material) existence, the only refuge and happiness is to seek our Essence, the Ultimate Treasure in us, which is independent of time and space and never succumbs to the degeneration and degradation matter, by nature, is heir to.

What could be more relevant and more appropriate to our times, or any time for that matter, than the idea that in this brief journey on the fleeting, yet infinite river of time one may indeed stand a chance to become conscious of, and perhaps even find within himself/herself, That which is not subject to time?

Vraje Abramian
December 2009
Los Angeles

INTRODUCTION

If you be wise, in words you won't get lost,
but ponder that secret to these lines we confided, and passed.
—Attar[7]

All happiness is a mirage in this domain,
seek that happiness Abu Saeed was given.
—Rumi[8]

For the material world to be, and continue being, consciousness must be embodied.

Throughout time, human intellect has made efforts to explain what caused us to "leave" that dimensionless ocean of absolute being and "come" here, the domain of space and time, a place of relativity, a battleground for complementary opposites.

In one favorite Sufi version, the Almighty Allah created heaven and earth and all creatures. He then fashioned us and not only breathed in us, but gave us the potential to contact this life force in our hearts; a favor no other creature on earth is granted.

Consciousness may appear in innumerable forms, but in human form, It can contemplate Itself. God then declared, "I am a treasure, and would like to be discovered!"[9] After which He told us, his breath given form, "Now you are with me in obedience, go, experience and realize my Love, and when It brings you back to me, we will meet not just as Lord and liege, but also as Lovers."

---

7 MKN, p. 11.

8 *Divan of Shams*, p. 335, no. 824; *see*, *Nobody Son of Nobody*, translated by Vraje Abramian, Prescott, Arizona: Hohm Press, 2001.

9 The Qor'aan.

To some, who were not too eager to leave, He said, "Worry not, for if in the midst of all my treasures in heaven and on earth, you still choose me, I will appear in your midst and bring you home, to Me."

And we began this game of hide and seek, where the One takes forms, becomes many, and falls in love with likeables, till he/she finds the way to the Loveable, the formless Self.

When we dream, our waking mind is asleep, our dreaming mind is busy dreaming, and then there is the one who witnesses the whole affair. It is said that if this potential in us "awakens," rather than remaining the overruled, passive witness to our mind's follies, we begin to understand our own condition and those of others.[10]

Sufi Poetry

Away from You, it is the perfumed memory of our union
lingering in my heart
that keeps me alive.
You are this perfume my love,
without You, my very soul would cease to be.

—Attar[11]

Like a donkey in the mud, mind gets stuck in this Affair;
the story of this love, only love can tell.

—Rumi[12]

In the last half-century or so, one of the bestselling poets in the West has been a 13th-century Persian Muslim mystic from

[10] For more on this see: Prabhavananda, Swami and Frederick Manchester. *Upanishads, the Breath of the Eternal*, Hollywood, Calif.: Vedanta Press, 1983, pp. 34-35.

[11] EN, p. 114, nos. 74-75.

[12] *Masnavi Manavi*, Book I, part 6. Personal translation by Vraje Abramian.

Khorasan[13]: Jalaloddin Mohammad Balkhi, known internationally as Rumi. There may be many reasons why: one could be the similarity between his times and ours. Rumi's times witnessed cataclysmic changes brought about by the invasion of most of Asia by Mongol tribes united under Temujin, whom the world knows as Chengiz Khan. These were nomadic people who often lived by the law of the sword, raiding each other for pillage and slaves. Ancient cities went to ruin overnight and their rich and poor were reduced to slavery under a people who found cities irritating obstacles to horsemanship. Once in possession of large tracts of conquered lands, they turned on each other and matters only got worse. They succeeded in one aspect rather well though, to the huge masses who lived under their rule and comprised the eastern half of the Muslim Empire, life's impermanence was demonstrated daily, making worldly values somewhat irrelevant. A surge in inner traditions, Sufism in particular, was a natural response to the vacuum thus created. In this sense the Mongol invasion became a "destructive construction," or a "constructive destruction."[14]

In our times, consumerism has half-wittedly promoted a cult of self worship which has become the dominant religion in most cultures regardless of the locally professed tradition/religion. But self-centered sensual indulgence finally degrades us to the lowest denominator and only highlights that vacuum which lack of true substance is. In a parallel development, the post-industrial era is demonstrating the folly of expecting sense in a world where manufacturing and consuming weaponry has become the mainstay of our global, industrial "civilization." We are seemingly embarked

---

13 Khorasan: Today, the northeastern Iranian province of Khorasan borders Afghanistan. In the nineteenth century, it denoted a much vaster region, which included western Afghanistan, as well as a major part of Trans-Oxanian Central Asia: present-day Tajikistan, Turkmenistan, Kazakhstan and Uzbekistan.

14 Danner, Victor. *Ibn Ata'Allah: The Book of Wisdom (The Classics of Western Spirituality)*, Paulist Press, 1978, p. 14. *Also see*: Austin, R.W. J., *Bezels of Wisdom, Ibn Al' Arabi (The Classics of Western Spirituality)*, Paulist Press, 1980, pp. 14-16.

on a self-destructive course, and to go from one day to the next, the thinking human needs a good measure of divinely-inspired humor and inner strength.

And Sufi masters' words, no matter in what garb they are dressed, point to a still, luminous center, not subject to human folly, but a witness to his/her final worth and triumph; a space in which the wretched find solace and the hopeful, affirmation.

Sanai, Attar and Rumi

When the young Jalaleddin's family was leaving Balkh ahead of the Mongol onslaught, his father Bahaoddin made a point of visiting every mystic on the way and asking for blessings. It is said that Attar told him that his boy would one day become the guiding light of his time and gave Jalaleddin a copy of *Asrar-nameh* (*The Book of Mysteries*), which in due course was to become his favorite book.[15]

Rumi uses more than a few pieces of Attar's works as the basis of some of his poems in *Divan-e Shams-e Tabriz*, and whenever Attar is mentioned he is given reverence reserved for those with the highest spiritual attainment. He also says the following about Sanai and Attar:

> Whoever understands Attar will be able to fathom Sanai, and whoever
> understands Sanai will be privy to my teachings. Sanai and Attar were
> both great ones on this path; while they often spoke of separation, I often
> speak of union.[16]

---

[15] Some scholars find Rumi's *Masnavi* similar to *Asrar-nameh* in construct. *See:* Babak, Ahmadi. *Four Studies of Tazkarat-ol Oliya*. Tehran, Iran: Nashr-e Markaz Publishing Company, P.O. Box 14155-5541, 1998, p. 154; *also see: Fihi Ma Fihi* (Persian), *In It Is What's In It*, Meeras-e Derakhshan-e Molana Jalaeddin Mohammad Molavi Series, foreword and editing by Hosein Heydarkhani (Moshtaq-Ali), 3rd edition. Tehran, Iran: Sanai Publications, 2002, p. 32. Personal translation by Vraje Abramian.

[16] DIV, Dr. Kadkani, pp. 36-37.

Again, he is quoted saying:

> The seven cities of love Attar traversed,
> the corner of the first alley we yet have to turn.
> Attar was the soul and Sanai the eyes,
> trailing behind them both have we arrived.[17]

Dr. M.R.S. Kadkani, the editor of some of the most recent, and most reliable, works of Attar (and many other Iranian mystics and poets), sees Iranian mystic poetry as a "...triangle made of Sanai (d 1150), who establishes the tradition, Attar (d 1221?), who elaborates, and Rumi (d 1273), who perfects" this ecstatic dialog about, and with, the Divine, with Hafez categorized in a class of his own.[18] Before Sanai, mystics, notably Sheikh Abu-Saeed Abil-kheir,[19] used spontaneous verse and rhymed prose to enliven their teachings and gatherings, but Sanai was the first to establish Sufi poetry as a genre of its own.[20]

Though often not as polished, Attar's word is deeply colored by the depth and intensity of his personal experience and the resulting urgency of his message:

> Had this lunacy not saved my sanity,
> I would have, long ago, lost my mind
> to the mysteries it is privy to.[21]

His own opinion of his poetry and of himself as a poet is rather revealing. Though he calls his poetry "The Persian Psalms (of

---

17 DIV, p. 37, Qazi Noor-Allah.

18 MKN, (Dr. M. R. S. Kadkani, editor). Tehran, Iran: Sokhan Publications, 1995, pp. 17-20.

19 See: *Nobody, Son of Nobody*, translations by Vraje Abramian, Prescott, Arizona: Hohm Press, 2001.

20 MKN, p. 17.

21 MKN, p. 22.

David)"[22], he is quick to let us know: "this talk is nothing but the surface, as a true one, you should seek the Depth, if you spend your life in words and discussion, when will you be able to do this Work?"[23]

And, speaking to his "heart":

> . . . though poetry can point to perfection, if you look carefully
> it is but a cover. Should you know a hair's breadth about this Affair,
> you won't make speeches nor write.
> Poetry I see as your idol, Attar, and thus you are nothing but an idol worshipper.[24]

Attar confesses that two powers drive him to write:

> . . . though silence is golden in all worlds
> two guardians goad me to speak
> from the day before the first day: this love in my soul,
> and the Beloved, from whom at every breath
> comes a command to string together these words.[25]

And finally he declares:

> . . . I speak only of Haqq.
> May I then be called the storyteller of Haqq.[26]

---

22 MN, p. 449, no. 7144.

23 EN, p. 400, nos. 6411-6413.

24 Ibid., p. 400, nos. 6414-6416.

25 MN, p. 453, nos. 7230-7238.

26 Ibid., p. 454, nos. 7244-7245. Haqq, "The Truth," one of the names of the Lord Almighty.

Historical Details

It is generally agreed among his biographers that Attar's name was Mohammad (Abu-Hamed Mohammad-ebne Ibrahim). He went by Farideddin, then Farid, and finally Attar as his pen name. He was born in the year 1119(?) in Kadkan, near Neyshaboor, Khorasan, Iran's eastern-most province. The village still stands today and is said to have been an important area since pre-Islamic (Zoroastrian) days.[27] Attar was killed during the Mongol invasion of Khorasan in 1221(?).

"Attar" means perfumer/herbalist in Arabic. This term, even today denotes an herbalist and "traditional" doctor in Persian. His father was an herbalist and Attar followed in his profession. His relative financial independence gave him the possibility to avoid entanglements with, and dependence on, rulers and courts. He married and had children, but details about his life are sketchy. Spiritually Attar shows the deepest respect to Sheikh Abu-Saeed Abil-kheir, Sheikh Abol-Hasan Kharaqani[28] and Bayazid Bastami.

> . . . The core of my being is drunk of this wine
> for through Abu-Saeed my cup of love has come.[29]

In Jami's "Nafahat-ol Ouns,"we hear Rumi, speaking to his disciples on his final day, saying:

> . . . be not sad about my pending departure
> for Mansour Hallaj after 150 years appeared
> to Attar and took him as his disciple . . .[30]

---

27 MKN, p. 23. Kadkan also happens to be Dr. Kadkani's hometown. Personal translations by Vraje Abramian.

28 *See: The Soul and A Loaf of Bread.* Translated by Vraje Abramian, Prescott, Arizona: Hohm Press, 2010.

29 MKN, p. 27. Personal translation by Vraje Abramian.

30 Jami, Nooreddin Abdorrahman. Nafahat-al Uns, 5th edition. Dr. Mahmood Abedi. Tehran, Iran: Sokhan Publications, 2007, p. 464. Personal translation by Vraje Abramian.

Based on a poem, which contains very specific terms and references reserved for one's Pir (Master), and which is dedicated to an aloof Khorasani adept and Sufi master, Sheikh Saadeddin Abolfazl-ebne Rabbib, Dr. Foroozanfar believes that Attar was indeed devoted to this mystic.

> . . . today, Khaje Saadeddin is the heart—
> for his heart is the blazing sun of our times.
> By truth, he is the pole star of all the saints,
> the special one in the court of the One.
> Through direct light granted by the Prophet,
> the religion and all its principles he has mastered.
>
> All the secrets in the Qor'an are known to him,
> for the absolute secret is not withheld from him.
> May I receive a grain from his mountain of grace,
> may my heart be lit by his light.[31]

True to form, Attar's personal details are sketchy, this does not, however, diminish the fact that he is a household name in many Persian-speaking homes, and that his word has nourished generations of people on the Path. It would perhaps be best to defer to Dr. Badeeozzaman Foroozanfar (d 1970) here, who says of him:

> Though he is one of the most famous characters in Persian literature,
> very little is known about Attar. He is one of those who were ahead of
> their times, and ours as well. They belong to an era in the future which
> human evolution and refinement may someday lead to.[32]

---

[31] DIV, p. 20. Personal translation by Vraje Abramian.

[32] EN, pre-content leaf. Personal translation by Vraje Abramian.

The Sufis: Contemplative Islam

> God was, and there was nothing with Him,
> and He is now as He was.
> —Ibn Ata'Allah[33]

It is said that in the great speed of the secular world, headed towards death, the contemplative misfit promotes the eternal. The Sufis certainly promote the eternal. They are the practitioners of the esoteric tradition within Islam. Occasionally they have been depicted as sects outside of Islam; whereas if anything, they should be classified as Muslims (those who have surrendered to the will of their Creator) who strive to maintain the teachings as guidelines in their daily conduct.

In the Hadith it is said that:

> . . . one's faith does not approach perfection
> until and unless, one loves That which one knows not
> more than all that one knows.[34]

Asceticism, renunciation, contemplative life, and in general mysticism, is seen by some as escapism[35] and Sufism has its critics. However, a quick glance at the more well-known Sufi orders will easily convince anyone that the practitioner has often been required to contribute, be active in his/her community and be

---

33 Danner, Victor. No. 37, p. 55.

34 Kaseb, Azizollah, editor. *Kashkool-e Sheikh Bahai* (by Bahaoddin Mohammad Abdol-Samad Amoli —known as Sheikh Bahai, d 1606AD/984AH), 9th edition, Goli Publications, Tehran, 2007(1385), p. 339. Personal translation by Vraje Abramian.

35 For an analytical study of the place of the contemplative in human community, *see*: Schuon, Frithjof. Appendix C: "The Universality of Monasticism…" in *Merton & Sufism, the Untold Story*, (edited by Rob Baker and Gray Henry), pp. 319-334.

an upright citizen in general. Purely monastic traditions never evolved in Islam.

A wise one said:

> This world is a place of suffering.
> One who runs after it, tortures himself;
> one who drags behind, tortures others.[36]

The famous adage in Sufi lore, *Del be yar-o dast be kar*[37]/ "Hands to work and heart to the Beloved," clearly attests to their dislike for idleness and to their firm belief in "being in this world but not of it." If the Sufis escape from anything, it is the bigotry of those who make of religion a platform for worldly ambitions. Every other page in the history of Sufism, and mysticism in general, contains heartrending accounts of persecutions and martyrdom of adepts who are branded as heretics by a priestly hierarchy weary of losing its livelihood.

Esoteric and Exoteric Traditions

When a mystic, spiritual teacher, gains public renown s/he might give sermons to the general public while continuing with the disciples whose professed priority is spiritual growth. Once the teacher passes away, often within a generation or two, the stories of his/her life and teachings are adopted by the mainstream forming the foundation of organized religion. Exoteric traditions thus formed, often have literal interpretations, and adopt rituals to commemorate the teacher's life and teachings. A professional religious class comes into existence. This priestly class has a major function on which its livelihood depends: performing rituals denoting birth, marriage, death, etc. Often they strive to maintain as much of the teachings as the power structure and the populace find convenient

[36] Kaseb. *Kashkool-e Sheikh Bahai*, p. 305, personal translation by Vraje Abramian.

[37] Persian.

and accommodating to the status quo. The popular image of the teacher is soon cast in the same mold as well, doing away with all the potentially inconvenient "eccentricities" of the now safely buried and mythologized person.

Baptism (initiation) becomes just another ritual performed in the name of the teacher, with the explicit, or implicit, guarantee of "salvation."

Should the teacher leave a successor behind to continue initiating, the esoteric tradition continues through the living teacher. Initiation here means that, through the agency and protection of the Perfect Master, a human being, who is a creature of yesterdays and tomorrows and has no eye for the present, is unhinged for a breath and splashes in the Eternal Presence getting a taste of limitless being.[38] This experience is considered a "second birth," or dying while still living.[39] The individual then begins a journey and grows in his spiritual capacity under the Master's guidance, in time becoming an insider to life, as it were, rather than always being impressed and ruled by matter, the shell, the form that veils the essence.

All mystic poetry is a depiction of this Affair according to the individual's experience, an effort to verbalize the unspeakable beauty of that Beloved aside from whom no one and nothing has true existence.

Gradually, the conditioned, lower mind—which thrives in this material world of "life eat life"—loses its hold on the seeker's consciousness till finally, through grace from above and the guidance of the Perfect Master, the individuated, embodied consciousness

---

[38] Any experience of limitlessness, or the limitless, is by definition outside the domain of everyday, standard human mind, which is a calculating and orientating tool based on information provided by our five senses, five *limited* senses. Obviously what mind cannot contain, it cannot explain, thus mysticism, mystics, mystery schools, etc.

[39] *See*: Charan Sing Ji, Huzur Maharaj. *Die to Live*. Beas, Punjab, India: Radha Soami Satsang Publ., 1979.

triumphs against all odds inherent in this lowest region and rejoins its Origin.

> O' Love, grant me annihilation,
> shatter the pitcher of my existence;
> what need can one have of it
> who has dissolved in The Ocean?
>
> —Hosein-ebne Mansour, Hallaj[40]

The perfect human thus produced, no matter where or when, encourages us to look for the treasure hidden in our essence, our highest potential. These perfect ones can affect lives in places far away and in times yet to come, for time and space do not pose the usual obstacles to them:

> Many who walk on earth and therefore are seen as alive
> are very much dead,

---

[40] Hosein-ebne Mansour, known as Hallaj, was born in 9th century in the southwestern province of Fars in Iran. In an ecstatic state, he declared, "Anal Haqq," I AM THE TRUTH, and not surprisingly was singled out by the religious establishment in Baghdad and eventually tortured to death in 922 immediately becoming the most celebrated Sufi martyr. His last statement was, "For the seeker, fulfillment is to be brought to union with the One he seeks."(Translation by Vraje Abramian). After that he tried to recite from the Qor'an (verse 18, al-Shouri), but could only go as far as, "Those, whose belief is not firm, seek in haste . . . " before he was silenced. *See*: Masoomi, Reza. *Arefaneha, Jami az Oqianoose Beekarane Erfan (Selections of Mystic Poetry, a Cup from the Infinite Ocean of Gnosi)* 6th edition. Tehran, Iran: Nashre-Eshare Publications, 1991. *Also see*: Ahmadi, Babak. *Four Studies of Tazkarat-ol Olya.* (Biography of the Saints.) Tehran, Iran: Nashr-e Markaz Publishing Company,1998. First Issue, p.189. *See also*: Abramian, Vraje, translator. *The Soul and a Loaf of Bread. The Teachings of SheikhAbol-Hasan of Kharaqan.* Prescott, Arizona: Hohm Press, 2010, pp. xix-xx.

while many who are presumed dead because their bodies
were buried
are very much alive . . .

—Sheikh Abol-Hasan of Kharaqan[41]

The suffering and the ecstasy of the individual soul, the drop that is still caged but has heard the sound of the ocean in a most secret "dream,"and the trials and tribulations it will go through before it can join its Beloved Origin, is said to be the highest pleasure and main reason for God's individuating and descending to his creation—his lila, the Divine play—

I was a hidden treasure
and I wished to be known,
so I created humankind.[42]

I created the world for you,
and you for Myself.[43]

Mystics in Islam

On the farthest boundaries of the Muslim empire, i.e., Khorasan, in easternmost Iran of the time, at a safe distance from the heavy-handed orthodoxy of Baghdad, esoteric Islam and what was left of ancient, local, pre-Islamic initiatory traditions blended and created that branch of Sufism which would be known as the School of Khorasan, the school of ecstatic love for the Divine. It would

41 Kadkani, Dr. Mohammad Reza Shafiee. *Neveshte-bar-darya, az miras-e erfani-e Sheikh Abol Hasan-e Kharaqani. Scripture on the Sea, from Spiritual Legacy of Sheikh Abol Hasan of Kharaqan.* Tehran, Iran: Sokhan Publications, 1988, p. 344, no. 1051, translation by Vraje Abramian.

42 "Hadith," International Association of Sufism Publication, San Rafael, CA, vol. xv, no. 2, p.17.

43 Ibid.

produce such luminaries as Hallaj, Teyfur Abu-Yazid Surushan al-Bastami (Bayazid of Bastam), Sheikh Abu-Saeed Abil-kheir, Sheikh Abol-Hasan of Kharaqan and Sheikh-ol Eshraq Sohravardi.[44]

The pre-Islamic, initiatory Iranian traditions, often referred to as "Tariqh-e Khosravan," The Royal Path, were not openly mentioned after Islam, but unmistakable references to these traditions remain standard symbols in Khorasanian, and by extension, all Persian Sufi lore to this day.

Here, "Pir-e Moqhan," or The Pir, the Elder of the Magi, denotes the Master; "Deyr-e Moqhan," or "Kharabat-e Moqhan," is a monastery, or a drinking place where a certain "Sharab," wine, is served which releases those looking for spiritual uplift from their lower self and grants them visions of their Beloved.[45]

Attar, one of the most prolific Sufi writers, is also one of those through whose work runs the unmistakable thread of ancient Persian mysticism and myth.

The Sufi Worldview

> Love hints, it doesn't reason, sell your heart to it.
> That is the best deal here.
> Let your heart climb out of that grave which is your ego
> into the light of Love.
> That is the only pilgrimage here. —Attar[46]

---

44 *See* Abramian, Vraje. *The Soul and a Loaf of Bread*, Prescott, Arizona: Hohm Press, 2010, p. xix. The other school of Sufi thought is known as that of Baghdad, which leans towards Jonaid's and Ibn Arabi's teachings. For a comprehensive study of the Sufis, *see:* Dr. Javad Nurbaksh's Foreword, pp. xv-xxxix, and "The Rise and Development of Persian Sufism" by Dr. S.H. Nasr, pp. 1-18, in *Classical Persian Sufism: From Its Origins to Rumi,* edited by Leonard Lewisohn, 1993.

45 *See*: Razi, Dr. Hashem. "Hekmat-e Khosravani," *The Royal Wisdom from Zoroaster to Sohravardi*. Tehran, Iran: Behjat Publications, 1979. *Also see:* Pournamdarian, Taqi. *The Vision of Simorqh: Attar's Poetry, mysticism and thoughts.* Tehran, Iran: Institute for Humanities and Cultural Studies, 2007.

46 DIV, p. 190, no. 105.

In the Sufi cosmology, while intelligence/curiosity is a primary asset, and propels the aspirant to ever newer horizons, a self-righteous, arrogant intellect is a hindrance. Folk stories about how Sufi masters threw books (bookish intellect) in the water, and turned the person's attention in the direction of the inner, living source of knowledge are recurring themes in Sufi biographies.

Knowing the Infinite is not possible by one's finite, limited mind; falling in love with, and at the end becoming one with the One, might be. The Sharia, the prescribed daily conduct of a Muslim in his/her worldly affairs, provides conditions which, in addition to guaranteeing a platform for common law, make spirituality probable. Being pious and trying to find one's way to heaven, while socially preferable to giving full reign to one's animal tendencies, is, at best, an insincere barter compared to loving, simply because the One is so lovable. Uncovering love, placed in trust in the human heart on the day before the first day, makes a human worthy of the name, and striving to return it to its source, the Beloved, provides substance and purpose in human life.

> O marvel! A garden among the flames. My heart has
> become capable of all forms.
> A meadow for gazelles and a monastery for Christian
> monks. . . . The Tables of the
> Law and the book of the Koran . . . I profess the religion
> of Love, and whatever
> direction its steed may take, Love is my religion and my
> faith.[47]
>
> —Ibn Arabi

In the journey towards the truth that which is hearsay and is not personal experience, gained under the guidance of the Master,

[47] Corbin, Henry. *Alone with the Alone: Creative Imagination in the Sufism of Ibn Arabi.* 6th edition. Bollingen; Princeton University Press, 1998, p. 135.

is a hindrance. And Love leads; that Love which commands obedience beyond personal gain, labels, dogma, popular approval, or disapproval, and finally beyond the speculating, calculating mind, which facilitates our worldly survival but hinders surrender to That which it is not equipped to grasp.

> What is human heart?
> The Emperor's favorite trophy,
> and the Emperor,
> whose hunting ground is this universe,
> is always on the trail of his trophy.
>
> — Attar[48]

A Tale

A tiny sparrow came to the Master once and declared rather despondently, "Nothing else has worked for me: I have to know God!" Upon which the Master told the bold seeker to go drink the ocean yonder and return. And our hero immediately flew there, and drank a few drops, before returning to the Master, even more agitated.

Master now said, "Why don't you try to fall in Love with God with all your heart? For in this affair your heart is privy to secrets your head can only deny."

The sparrow heard, as if for the first time in its life, and it never "knew" how that happened, so it could, of course, never explain it to other sparrows.

They say this bird one day screamed very loudly and vanished into its own ecstasy and has not since been heard of!

❧

"God was and there was nothing with Him"; and Masters say that once all distraction burns in the fire of love, multiplicity disappears and one realizes that, "He is now as He was."

---

[48] DIV, p. 197, no. 103. Personal translation by Vraje Abramian.

Every human is a mystery in that personal space where no one else exists, a hermetically sealed container whose key is in the hands of the Perfect Master whom one cannot describe! The only sign is that in his presence thoughts slow down, and should He wish so, stop. To explain the "Pir," the Master, is an impossibility, for in his august Presence, should He wish so, a certain wine is served which snatches one away from oneself; that penny-wise, argumentative, know-it-all self which is full of worldly cleverness and has forgotten, for lifetimes, to breathe out!

And our sheikh's words are most certainly perfumed by this wine.

May these renditions of a few of Attar's poems bring you that perfumed wine which causes a certain tipsiness whence a nostalgic heart may begin missing anew the ancient love trusted to it on the day before the first.

My dear darling,
before you were brought into existence
the Emperor lay himself a treasure
somewhere deep within your being;

should He so desire,
He recovers it,
should He not, He leaves it be.
Why should you presume to know
why, wherefore or whence?"

—Attar[49]

Vraje Abramian
November 2012
Los Angeles

[49] EN, p. 155, nos. 105-108. Personal translation by Vraje Abramian.

THE POEMS

This sweet sorrow granted at love's door
is the true treasure buried in our soul
a particle of it will bestow upon you more
than the two worlds could ever hope for.

—Attar

1. In the name of the One
whose sovereignty never diminishes
and in whose praise speech vanishes,
the One whose absolute domain
would suffer not a hair's loss in its eternity
were creation to vanish in its entirety.

2. Glory is You of whom no particle is empty
though no trace of You can be found.

3. In that ocean where all creation is but a drop
what could this existence of ours mean?
If you leave this self behind for a moment
in your forehead you will hear, "You are Mine."

Revealed here are the psalms in Persian,
but to understand them one needs the seal of the Sovereign.
Lord, let Attar be erased from the scene,
and let these be Your and not his lines.

4. If both worlds and all in them disappear
worry not
but do take a breath in "Huzur," in God's Presence,
for what you will mourn for an eternity to come
will be those breaths you failed to take in Presence.

5. Embracing You is a secret affair,
whoever declares it is not sincere.
My heart is a moth aflame in that love
to which my mind can only be a stranger.

6. There is a candle in the invisible realm—
a candle neither bright nor dim.
I am a moth afire in its flame—
that's where my words find their shine.

7. O' companions come
let's speak about our secret
about this ancient heartache.
Like strings on a harp
every vein in my body sings of this love.
I would say so much more
but this pain refuses to be spoken of.

8. Hidden in these lines
are gathered secrets from both worlds.
Should reading ever lead one to the Way
then read in earnest and learn their import,
for like flickering lights burning in your chest
they will guide you to "Huzur," God's Presence.

9. Hear me well my dear
you are the Beloved,
but should this secret be openly declared
your very life will disappear.
Thus, veils within veils cover you
from your own self and from your kind,
yet within a thousand veils in a thousand ways
you and your Beloved are eternally embraced.

10. Story

A man saw Majnoon and Leylee
seated in an oasis face to face.
"What an amazing sight," he thought,
"they ever lived in separation, this can't be right."

"O' but this can't be wrong," said Majnoon,
"for we are never separate.
We were lovers
before the two worlds were yet thought of!"

11. "When I sent forth the human
it was my beauteous glory
that I made manifest,"
says the Beloved.

12. A human is a handful of dirt
with some air in it for breathing;
the soul is the treasure buried there deep
with the dragon of the body guarding it.

13. Virtue is—
to gain intimacy
then forever to see soul first
and form last.

14. Humans are the most fortunate of all
for both worlds are but contained in the human soul.
Whoever finds his way to his soul
will find the Beloved there.
From every heart a secret path leads to the Emperor—
the One who can never be seen without—
for He lives within you, in your very heart, says the Master.

15. What could the purpose of it all be without the human?
Until the human was created there was no path to God.
The human is this path and the key to both worlds
and the angels therein, for he contains them all.
Though in dirt is this jewel now mired
no fear, for by the True Jeweler it is admired
and when the philosopher's stone is applied
true human's worth is finally brought to light.

16. To repent is—
to disregard all that's offered here
and to move our hopes from here to There.

17. Salvation is—
to find a way to your goal
through the secret passage in your soul.

18. This handful of dirt was brought to life
by the grace of light
to become that which mind can fathom not.
The secret the creation is denied
shines on the human forehead like broad daylight.
The favorite of the manifest world
the secret of the command
such is true human's true might.
This description in lovers' language
suits the human just right,
but those lost in this world or the next
would fathom this not.

19. Your heart's lineage is not of Adam and Eve,
nor can your soul
on earth or in heavens find her reprieve.

20. O' miraculous bird of heavens beyond
your story begins on the day before the first day.
"Jaam-e Jam," the all-seeing cup of Jamsheed
the great wise king
is a treasure box buried deep in your heart.

21. Like one caught in a whirlpool
you are a dreamer stuck in a dream.
One day when you finally enter this ocean
relieved from this vessel made of your dreams
the ocean will show you
who in truth you are.

22. There's a mystery beyond all mysteries—
a light brighter than all other lights.
Remember, while attending to all your affairs,
there is a task above all other tasks.

23. Do you not carry that jewel
all angels were commanded to bow to?
Worry not then if your body ends up six feet under
for your soul is from above, from Pure Wonder.

24. I saw my existence and it was a shadow
cast aground by that sun that is my Beloved.
I reached to catch the hem of his robe
and I saw his hand in my sleeve.
Whoever realizes the mystery in this story
is greatly fortunate and may taste victory.

25. When there is One
who is All there is
how can this thought called me
exist?

26. Whoever came into being
is like unto a dewdrop separated from the ocean;
that which it used to be
is what it searches after.

27. Poverty of the soul is—
to want nothing in both worlds
but the way out of this waywardness.

28. Story

A tiny bird was chirping
as King Solomon and his party passed
and the King said:
"That little creature just said
that half a date it has eaten all day
and that has been enough,
and so to run after worms underground
would be a greedy affair.
Learn from our little teacher—
whoever finds worldly greed degrading
will turn into pure light though his body turn
to dust."

29. When the sun rises
both the palace and the mud hut are lit,
but one who walks naked in poverty
is warmed more quickly.

30. Dignity is—
to abandon that lowliness
which is your ego
and to look for your Self
in the Bestower of Dignity.

31. There is an Affair
beyond youth and age
beyond life and death,
a secret beyond all veils,
an eternal being, beyond existence
and nonexistence.

32. I was born in the same body
with the dog of my ego,
and my lifetime suffering has been
to teach it about the spirit.

33. When a wayfarer mixes up the identities—
his own and that of his donkey
and makes his purpose in life the comfort of his beast—
he comes to know remorse and dies of grief.

34. We are all porters here
carrying this sack of filth around night and day.
Whether one commands armies and countries
or is a man of learning full of studies,
if only ego runs your affairs
you are not much better than a beast.

35. Story

A lunatic who made his home in a cemetery
witnessed final prayers for one corpse too many.
Turning to the crowds he declared in his genuine wit,
"Why not say a farewell prayer
for this entire world and all in it
and get it over with?"

36. Everyone here journeys in his own dream:
harmony or chaos are our choices here
heaven or hell they are called in hereafter.
When breathing one's last on this side
a heart resting in contentment and trust
will find the same when it crosses over.

37. The worldly man is less than a dog
for dogs eat their fill and pass,
but the greedy never tires of wanting and is crass,
and though tomorrow has not been promised him
he worries about a hundred years in advance.

38. Story

A grand sire full of borrowed dignity
was passing by a public outhouse
whereupon he picked up his robe and held his nose.
A lunatic was at hand. "Lovely gentleman," he said,
"Why turn up your nose at that which adorned your
table last night?
Sporting a full-fledged cemetery for a belly
lost in a sack of boiling blood and puss
you tear each other apart like mad dogs
and devour the meek like a pack of hyenas
dragging that sanctity that is this life in your filth,
then put on airs and turn up your nose at your
final product."

39. A mad one once asked the King,
"Which do you like better—
your gold or your deeds?"
"One who has tasted gold, can't help but like it," said
the King.
"Then why do kings leave their gold behind at death
and travel in the company of their deeds?"
said the one touched by sweet insanity.

39. 1 Story

Haroon, the great sultan, told Bohlool, the wise fool,
"Do let me know if you have some needs or some loans
to pay,
and I shall pay them and spare you their thorns."
"You don't have a penny of your own. You take from
others whatever you own.
And who has told you to steal from some and give to
others what's not yours?"
said Bohlool.

40. Whatever you collect here
chains you.
When that night arrives
which does not contain tomorrow's promise
one who possesses the least and knows peace
steps lightly and welcomes the release.

41. What calamity has befallen Adam and Eve's children?
One can neither complain nor calm remain
a mountain of dreams contained in a straw
taking birth one day in blood and pain
dying after a lifetime of desiring in vain.

42. Greed is—
to pile up that mountain
under which you'll be buried.

43. One who is stingy
is like unto a man sitting by an ocean of sweet water
worried that if today he drinks
tomorrow there will be less.

44. To be content is—
to see blessings in all things
and within them to behold the One
who gives all blessings.

45. Arrogance is—
to blow on red-hot iron and
to preach bad behavior to a demon!

46. Story

When the world was given Alexander in conquest
death appeared at his door and cut short his quest.
"Prepare a box and dig a hole at my city's entrance,"
said the sovereign with a bleeding heart,
"... and when I die, leave my two empty palms
out of my coffin facing upwards
for the whole world to see and to mourn this bitter loss.
Empty-handed I came and empty-handed I leave thus."

47. That which is called success here
hangs around your neck when you die
and it is time to swim across.

48. If you wear the sun for your crown
you will still have no choice
but to surrender it in time.

49. How can one remember death
and still cause torment and be unjust?
Some days death clutches at my heart,
yet other times I take solace in its approach
and find peace,
for from this dust bin
it heralds my soul's release.

50. A youth saw an old man bent by age
like a hideous bow.
"Come old man," he said in mirth,
"a piece of silver for your bow?"
"Save your silver young arrival
tomorrow you will get one for free," said he.

51. Story

A pious one said,
"The worldly man is like unto a manure roach—
all his life he packs manure together
rolling it in dirt till he gets to his home,
and then he has to leave it outside,
for the manure ball is too big by now
and his tiny hole defies his enormous catch."

52. You were nothing once
and will soon again be nothing.
Why not be nothing now as well?
What is a human?
A drop separated from the sea,
sorrows won't find it
if it drowns and loses itself in the Ocean.

53. When one dies
one of two things happens:
if he arrive filthy he is scrubbed,
if he arrive pure he is clothed in peace.

54. One who finds light in his heart here
cannot rise a dunce in hereafter.
Neither does one who here knows latrines only
rise a jurist in the afterlife.

55. Story

When God's own friend Abraham died
he was addressed by his Lord thus:

O' luckiest one of all
what in life for you was the most difficult?

"Sacrificing one's first-born, hearing one's father's
death groan,
walking through a pyre and dealing with life's ire
are all tortuous," he said, "And yet,
compared to death's throes they are but a satire."

So it is, said the Lord, and yet,
one who dies to himself while still alive
finds that peace which death cannot deprive.

56. Your body is a trap for a magical bird—your soul—
whom you refuse to acknowledge
until death arrives to set It free!

57. I found pain and confusion
when I fell into the illusion of existence;
not before my heart drowned in its own blood
could I drown in non-being
and discover a thousand pearls there.

58. Born to the unreal here
you have forgotten your reality.
If you could have a glance at your Self
you would scream in utter love.

59. Thousands of firmaments turn and toil
for someone like you to appear
and through every breath
move a step closer to your goal.

60. You are a heavenly bird
stuck in this dark well where you die
knowing neither heaven nor earth.
If you ignore the bones thrown to the dogs here
you might discover your wings
and leave this dark cell.

61. To be denied is—
to be given to worshipping one's body
and to forget one's soul.

62. My dear all you know is waking and sleep
all you worry about is life and death.
Your Lord is neither
now you may go back to sleep.
He is neither body nor mind
and He can't be named;
now enjoy your slumber!

63. The reason you've been told
that love for one's place of origin
is a sign of faith
is that in your place of origin, within your soul,
resides your Beloved.
You are your own Beloved
come back to your Self
do not search the world over
return within, to your Origin.

64. Let your soul learn about the inner meaning
and become a royal hawk worthy of the King's arm,
so one day when it hears the call of his special drum
it will take to its wings and fly home.

65. If here you do not refine your vision
you will die blind and rise blind hereafter.

66. O' slumbering one, should you be wise,
to your desires and wants you'd shut your eyes,
for it's your greed that brings your demise.
Wayfarers we are and in the eyes of a wayfarer
nothing in this flea market should deserve a second glance.

Trust the Giver in steadfast patience
for if He does not withhold from those who never
remember,
why would He withhold from those
who only in Him put their trust?

67. Story

When Adam realized the Secret of his task
after landing in this abode of sorrows,
for a lifetime he bitterly cried.
You are his child and there are tears here for you too,
yet that which accompanies you beyond is also found here.
Be awake then, for here you procure your pain and your
cure as well.

68. To pray—
after you have descended to this mud pit in shame—
is to seek your soul's way to its origin.

69. Here one cries at your funeral
because he is reminded of his own death.
Strive to discover the company of your own Self
to be prepared for the time when, for eternities,
you will be your own only company.

70. To live is—
to dare death
so as to break out of existence
and to arrive at Life.

71. Story

The great Sheikh of Mehne once was experiencing a contraction of the heart.
"Step outside," he said to his disciple,
"and bring in the first man you come across."
The attendant returned with an old man in trail.
"Speak to me of your life and times
mayhap it will make my heart expand," said Sheikh Abu-Saeed.
"May you be blessed," said the man.
"Yesterday morn, life gave me a son
whom in my jubilation I named Javeedanzad,
meaning forever alive, in our Zoroastrian tongue.
Today I performed his funeral, for last night he died,
and may the Sheikh live long."
And they both shed a few tears.

72. A perfect one said—
a wise one is not one who lives happily,
but one who dies with a happy heart
free from that which may hold him back.

73. Though a human here seems a handful of dirt
no dirt ever touches the Sun within.
One who doesn't behold that Sun
dies a blind bat.
A life not offered to its Beloved
is its own punishment.

74. You are a drop of morning dew—
only in the ocean you may be renewed.
Disappear into the Beloved if you want eternal life.

75. In the goblet of my soul
I was served this wine at dawn.
I found it too good for the likes of me,
so I keep it a secret from everyone
even from myself.

76. That which you have never lost
and know nothing about
but have always been looking for,
if someone were to ask you what it is,
what would your answer be?
Sit in solitude and stop this prattle in your mind
so you may perchance ponder
what your true desire is.

77. For many years riding the steed of wind
I searched the entire world for You.
You were sitting in my chest,
but in my proud ambitions
I had not a moment to contemplate my heart.

78. Out of the sanctum of eternity
you were dragged by illusions.
O' little droplet
why did you leave the ocean for the desert?

79. Tell me
how does one have to rattle your prison chains?
Having crept into your own trap
how long will you worship
your own delusion?

80. Wayfaring is—
to surrender your spot
to experience the orbit.

81. Someone asked a seafarer
to tell him of the wonders of the sea.
"The greatest wonder of all," said the sailor,
"is that in this vastness full of peril
any ship ever makes it ashore."

82. The alchemy practiced by the true ones
is to let your entire being become your heart,
and then fill it with this longing and pain—
the pain of wanting the One you can't explain.
Since neither on earth nor in heavens It can be found,
be still and contemplate your heart.
What else is there to speak about?

83. To be truly smart is—
to outsmart your clever mind.

84. Hidden from both worlds
a treasure sought in the place of mysteries—
the inner secret of the Perfect Human.

85. Show me one who is not absorbed in himself
and I'll reveal him the universe
he carries in his heart.

86. Loqhman the wise said,
"I have regretted a great deal
because of saying too much,
but never has silence brought
any regrets or heartaches."

87. How can you be contained?
How can the most wondrous bird of heaven be caged?
You are a seed sown on this earth—
once you begin to germinate
in both worlds you won't be contained.

88. To fall short is—
to spend the day just to arrive in the evening,
then to find it a trap made of your dreaming.

89. If you could be a king
wouldn't it be a pity to die a pauper?
While this whole world is an offering to you
would it not be a shame to die of hunger?

90. David, the prophet, asked his Creator
why humans had been created.
"So this hidden treasure, I Am,
may be discovered," he was told.

91. Bou-Ali Toosi, the great mystic, asked a knower,
"Is this journey from man to God or from God to man?"
"Neither," said the knower, "for if He is all there is,
and none other exists,
then this journey is from God to God!"

92. To speak words of substance
one needs to have Christ's lifegiving breath,
and like Mary
give virgin birth.

93. Story

Once while Jesus was passing by
a snake charmer was working his trade
trying to trick a huge snake into his basket.
"Three hundred years have I been around," said the beast,
"am I to become a prisoner to this thirty-year-old's tricks?"
When He saw it again, this time trapped and bound,
Jesus asked how, and the snake confided,
"I could have killed him, his charm wasn't his protection,
but he kept repeating my Beloved Lord's name
and in my delight and delirium I bought into his game.
I will sacrifice a hundred lives to the One
in whose name I was ushered into this place of blame."

94. A wise one asked one forlorn and lost in his search,
"How can you find that which you've never lost?"
"True, o' great one," he said, "but pray tell me
how can one be missing that which one's never lost?"

"It can neither be found nor lost.
Here, neither utterance nor silence seems right,
but the purpose is for you to arrive
where you are not just this, nor that, but both!"

95. Story

A man came to a wise one and said,
"For many years I have looked high and low;
many privations, many pains have I tasted,
but no door have I found to enter through."
The Sheikh said, "You have found that
which you have preferred and reached for,
for on this path, though we are deeply blind,
the Giver is as vastly knowing as He is kind,
and whatever in truth we are reaching for
that, and none other, are we allowed to find."

96. Story

A generous devotee asked the Lord for many days
to be honored and be sent a worthy guest
till in his heart he heard, "I have sent you a guest,
be prepared to receive him tomorrow morn."
He prepared and prepared and waited patiently,
but by nearly noon other than a stray dog
none else had stopped at his gate
and that, his servants had chased away promptly.
As he was preparing to complain copiously he heard,
"I sent you one of mine and you treated it unkindly."
The man searched and searched madly,
and finding the dog he cried and regretted bitterly
till the dog lifted its head and said,
"You asked for a guest and one was given,
but missed your gift since you had forgotten to ask for
proper vision."

97. Failure is—
to be blinded by appearances
and to make of oneself a living corpse.

98. Awaken before you die—
do not die while a corpse!

99. Hopelessness is—
to burden hearts already burdened
and to abandon those with whom you count.

100. Story

Sultan Mahmood one day
chanced upon an execution and pausing hastily
glanced at the man who was to be hanged summarily.
"O carrier of justice," shouted the man emboldened by
 death's gaze,
"here ten thousand are looking at my misery,
should there be no difference in their glance and that
 of a sovereign's?
What travesty dare stand in the way
should my king feign to look at me favorably?"
Mahmood was pleased,
paid his ransom and had him released.

101. Inside the shell of this body
your soul is seeking to become a pearl.
Yet, in this infinite ocean of life
though the Emperor is offering you a hand,
all you are intent on doing
is to ever remain on the land.

102. To be depressed is—
to see only a body
and to ignore your heart and soul;
to make a residence of the eye of the needle
then to feel out of place and complain of your prison.

103. Why would the One
who provides for those who deny him
withhold from one who lives in his remembrance?

104. Why do you fear returning to your Beloved
when if you take a single step
He will run from eternity to receive you?

105. Fear is—
to ignore the Protector
and walk in heaven in trepidation.

106. Everyday
a hundred calls come to you from the Friend,
but too self-indulged are you to acknowledge.

107. What do you think the moth pays
to enjoy, but for a moment,
the company of its beloved flame?

108. Safety is—
to wash your hands of yourself
and to see yourself a lifeless shadow.

109. Story

Someone asked Yahya the great mystic,
"Why did the Prophet, who had rulership over
both worlds,
say He wished He had never been born?"
"On a humble happy plain," said the elder,
"two nomads, a man and a woman,
had their tents pitched across.
In love with each other they lived in bliss
until their animals multiplied and they had servants.
Their humble tents then turned into palaces plush—
the lovebirds were separated thus, each in their kingdom,
each suffering and mourning the other's loss!
And they shall mourn and the world shall turn
until they surrender their crowns and return to their
humble plain
and find their lost love as humble nomads again."

110. You were cast to seek and cherish the Sultan,
yet here you are seeking grasslands to graze on.

110.1 The worldly are like mad dogs—
they devour this corpse of a world in their ignorance
and will tear apart anyone who suggests otherwise.

111. Jesus of Mary was asleep
his head resting on half a brick
when he opened his eyes
he saw Satan standing by.
"What brings this curse here?" he asked.
"The world belongs to me,
and that brick as well—
here I am, guarding my property," said he.
The Nazarene gave up the brick and bid the accursed
to leave.
"Now you are rid of me," said he, "and fare thee well."

112. Story

Bayazid, the great saint of Bastam, one morn
found a dog in his company and in disgust picked up his robe.
The dog whimpered, "Your affair is simple with me,
the uncleanliness I may cause can be avoided or washed,
but your affair with yourself, that is what you should worry about,
for though I am a stray dog despised by most
I have hidden no bones for lunch and my Provider I always trust.
Yet the great Bayazid, who commands everyone's blessing,
cannot go without casks of winter grain in his pantry."
Bayazid's heart was set on fire and he moaned,
"I do not deserve the company of your dogs, Lord,
how can I ever hope for your company?"

113. I am fed up with this mind,
an ant that needs a grain of wheat a week,
treacherously plotting to own every granary in sight.

114. Story

The Sheikh of Mehne
the great Abu-Saeed
was enjoying himself in a public bath.
"A pleasant place indeed," a companion said.
"That it is," said the Shiekh, "and here's why—
while one bathes
the only things one needs of this degrading world are
a borrowed towel around the waist and a water bowl,
neither of which one need possess."

115. Why run after desires and wants
and burn in jealousies and greed
when what we give our life to gather
we will leave behind
and to the winds scatter?

116. In this world of decay
find that which is not of this world
so you may live after you leave this world.
If you live for this, you'll find here death only.
Every moment a message comes from the Friend,
"You are a manifestation of the Deathless
why don't you know yourself?"

117. You have promised yourself to find It after life.
How can one find in death
that which he missed in life?

118. Story

Sheikh Abu-Saeed of Mehne,
the sultan of the path,
was asked by a bystander to intercede
and save from the constable's wrath
a man who, while being beaten severely,
was pleading to be spared
and took God's name repeatedly.
"How can I oblige, friend," said the saint,
"when only now and thus he is reminded of his God?"

119. Before you die,
should you be able to die but for a moment,
you will find within
far more than heavens and earths.

120. I am afraid of sinking in this ocean
so I busy myself with trinkets on the shore,
fattening my ego, starving my soul.

121. Unmindfulness is—
to see a locked gate
where there is only a curtain,
and end up left out in the rain.

122. O' worshipper of yourself
isn't it time for the demon you carry within
to prostrate itself?
Every breath taken in ego
adds to that dark smoke that settles in your chest.
Attar has revealed what he knows,
now then the decision is yours.

123. To carry a grudge is—
to make a prison of your heart
and to house a dragon in your chest.

124. To forgive is—
to relieve your soul's burden
to see trespass, yet to maintain your equity.

125. When I can find no sincerity in me
how can I look for it in others?

126. That which this world calls alchemy
is but God's Light upon the true heart.
Whoever It shines upon, be he an unlettered villager,
turns into Sheikh Abol-Hasan of Kharaqan;[1]
be he a King, he becomes Ebrahim Adham[2]
who abandons his throne
to gain that heart which, needless of either,
rules heaven and earth both.

127. Release me from myself Beloved
for with this self I am helpless.

128. There is a science
through which you find the spring of eternal life.
Once you do you may die aware and free,
and your very dust becomes the water of life!

---

1 Sheikh Kharaqani, the great 10th-century saint: see *The Soul and A Loaf of Bread: The Teachings of Sheikh Abol-Hasan of Kharaqan,* renditions by Vraje Abramian, Prescott, Arizona: Hohm Press, 2010.

2 Ebrahim Adham, a Bokharan ruler who abandoned his throne to enter the Path and became a great saint.

129. I have yet to find one
who can leave himself behind
so he can hear and understand
this story in my heart.

130. Even if both worlds were filled with keys—
this lock they cannot open.
Sell your clever mind and buy wonder—
that is the smartest barter available here.

131. In my long lives
everything I've done has brought regrets.
This humiliation I bear is because of me.
Without me I'd spring out of this prison and join
my Friend.
I am thus abandoning Attar
and will sit in this corner facing the wall.

132. Should you ever stop your mind from sifting water
you shall realize in a moment
that this entire world is deeply asleep.

133. Language is of the mind
which boils eternally,
but the story of the soul
is heard in silence only.

134. Sit face to face with yourself in solitude
and listen so as to hear.
Do not mind opinions,
struggle to experience certainty.

135. The fish that dares this ocean
severs its earthly ties
and learns the secret of the breath.

136. Control your breath every dawn,
and in this domain of veils and separation
you might still breathe with your Beloved;
otherwise one ends up just a no one.
Were the world to follow this advice
would it still be ruled by this chaos?

137. Creeds and religions are varied due to the
wayward mind—
where trust is needed, it breeds doubts.
When crude, mind withers one's life,
when refined, it imprisons one's soul.
It has to be kept in command for otherwise
in its clutches only ruination is to be found.
When Love finally rends one's heart
mind too receives its fair reward.

137.1 Sanai, the great poet, walking on a road
saw a washerman at his trade, while from a minarette nearby he heard
a muezzin making the morning prayer call.
"Not much difference between the two, for they are both after a coin or two,
though one is honest and does hard work while the other
is affecting a virtue he might not be possessed of," the great sage thought.

138. A seeker went to a master in China,
"Teach me about truth," he said.
"There are ten steps to truth," he replied.
"The first is to speak less
the other nine are heard in silence."

139. All existence appears as foam on the ocean of silence.
Let this passing affair not bring you arrogance,
for a wave from the same ocean may simply erase all this.
If today with silence you make friends
tomorrow in its bosom you'll find solace,
otherwise a world of regrets awaits once you leave this place.

140. In this prison of illusions be insignificant
vanish in this sea, be not even a drop.
All creation is a mirror reflecting God's face—
let the face be your delight
not the mirror.

141. While here, cease this scatteredness in your heart
for tomorrow in your grave, this would be very difficult.
Seek "Huzur," the Presence, here,
so there you will not feel lonely and out of place.

142. Keep your secret a secret
for your enemy is hiding in your shirt.
Attar was not revealed the secret
till he became his own enemy!

143. Since I am neither learned nor ignorant
I am spared the company of both;
since I have chosen silence
I am shunned by both listeners and speakers!

144. When the world is finally calm and asleep
be awake, alone, distant from yourself,
and let your heart call your Beloved.
That which one might receive on such a night
is unlike the trinkets we are here offered.

145. Silence is—
to refuse to entertain that
which is not the Beloved.

146. To tell one's story in this Affair is—
to attempt to speak of that
which can never be verbalized.

147. From the world of the hidden
if you have a sign
it's a shame to let it appear on your tongue,
for that which you lose thus
is very difficult to again come across.

148. If being with You is not to be my lot
then I'll spend this life longing for You.
As long as there's a single breath yet
it'll be spent in this remembrance.

149. Zekr is—
to derive healing from one's ailment,
and to dig a secret tunnel
from one's heart to one's soul.

150. A lifetime without a moment in God's Presence
is but a wasted chance.
If you exist to eternity
a moment spent in this Presence
is all you'll remember as life.

151. If the whole world turns on you
do not turn back, do not react.
Swim in this ocean of phenomena
but don't get wet.

152. The way out is—
to accept being naught
and once so, to be pleased with that which is
and that which is not!

153. Story

Abu-Saeed, that great mystic of yore, said to his disciples,
"Learn from the flour mill's grinding stone about the secrets of the Path,
ever turning, never displaying its works,
receiving coarse grain, offering in return refined nourishment,
always travelling, never moving from the center,
every breath occupied, not a moment is it idle."

154. To go on pilgrimage is—
to journey to the motionless center in your heart
and to drown there in the longing that you find.

155. Hope is—
to find happiness in the dew
while keeping the ocean
in your sight.

156. The great mystic, Shebli
one morn saw Satan on his way to the mosque,
"What has brought you here, o cursed one,
is it that you still harbor some hope?" he asked.
"O great Sheikh remember," said Satan sorrowfully,
"I was driven away by the One
whose divine action none can question,
and whose divine mercy one may always hope for."

157. What a bewildering amazement
that an ant unknowingly takes on the entire universe.
The more you advance on this Road
the more bewilderment assails you.

158. To fear is—
to imagine a shadow
then to wither in its shade.

159. The breeze of dawn
blows every particle of dust to ecstasy;
whoever received a robe of honor
received it at this hour.
Rise early and let your longing sigh
for nothing brings a human more joy
or may elevate one as high.

160. To have joy is—
to die to everything that will die tomorrow.

161. What is the sign of the Path?
That the farther you travel
the worse you become in your own eye.

162. If your heart is not deserving of your soul
how can it stand its light?
How long will you speak of your worth?
Pick up a handful of dirt and throw it up in the wind
and you will behold your substance and your worth.

163. I have travelled all and many roads,
yet I have not taken the first step.
Every moment I add to my worthlessness,
and though my hair has turned white
in my desires I am but yesterday's child.

164. Cause no one pain
and be patient with your load.
To your true home this is the shortest road.

165. Everything was issued from the One,
it's wise then to see the whole world as one;
otherwise, though you be mighty and fly very high,
at the end only dirt will cover you above and below.

166. The Beloved appeared in this marketplace
to behold himself.
He wanted a castle for himself
so He made the human.
He appeared as cotton and silk too
for humans to adorn His castle.
He came as the idol
and appeared as the idol worshipper too.

167. **Story**

To Khaje Nizam al-Molk—the King's prime minister,
a poor gardener from a poor province—brought as
 precious gifts
three cucumbers from the season's first picks.
The great vizir ate one, then another, and then the
 last one,
and giving the poor man thirty gold sovereigns sent him
 back to his town.
To his retinue he then turned and said,
"Those were bitter, very harshly bitter,
and should anyone have mentioned a word
it would've broken the poor man's heart.
Mind me not, good gentlemen, for I could not see him
 shamed."
On the day of judgment nothing carries more weight
than forbearing kindness to all of God's creatures.

168. Courtesy is—
to avoid friction and to uphold goodwill,
to mind the darkness in one's own shadow
and resolve not to give in to its evil.

169. One whose heart is empty of anger and want
is an ocean of truth,
draw near him.

170. In both worlds I am searching for the one
who has freed himself from belonging
to help me find an opening
from this prison house I was born in.

171. The world is full of light
but you are full of shadows.
Look for a Blessed One, for without a Master
you are a curse upon yourself.
Whether thorn or flower be his and be safe.
If you remember only this from Attar
you will have enough to last you forever.

172. If you want your estranged soul
to learn about this intimacy
seek the shelter of the Pir, the Master.
No blind wayfarer makes it home without a guide.

173. When the Absolute
in Essence manifests in the particle,
this particle is capable of changing others.
How or why
are not questions that interest the Absolute.

174. If you can't be a lover
then strive to gain the friendship
of a lover.

175. One who thirsts for inner meaning
must take shelter at the Master's feet.
The least one thus achieves in this world
is that he is not waylaid by its bandits.

176. Our Pir awoke at dawn
and left the mosque for the Tavern.
After a pitcher he told everyone,
"This drunkenness suits me fine
you should all try it sometime."
"We will hang this blasphemer," said the
self-righteous mob.
"A hundred thousand lives for that Beloved
at whose feet lovers offer their souls," said the Pir.
And walking up to the gallows
entered his Beloved's eternal meadows.
The story of Hallaj[3] has brought joy to every pure
heart since
and has guided Attar in his search for his goal.

177. Master said, "Your heart is an ocean of love
and the language of the soul is its language."

[3] Hallaj: Mansour Hallaj, the famous Sufi saint.

178. Every happy heart that I have come across
was in love with this affliction.

178.1 One who does not find his joy in this longing
will have to seek for contentment in that mound of dirt
piled upon one at the end here.

179. Beloved
grant those who deny You
their denial,
and those who come to You for heaven,
their heaven,
but pray, grace Attar's heart with that pain
that from You alone one may hope to gain.

This sweet sorrow granted at love's door
is the true treasure buried in our soul—
a particle of it will bestow upon you more
than the two worlds could ever hope for.
One bereft of this pain can hope for no cure.

180. Our Pir fled the monastery
and landed in the Tavern.
There in the midst of those lost to themselves
he surrendered reason and downed a full cup,
and seeing that which cannot be described
became a stranger to all there is.
It must be that the sun of the souls
unveiled Itself, revealing that meadow
where reason becomes a blind bat caught in the
    sun's light
and the soul turns into a butterfly.

181. If this sorrow enters your heart for a moment
you will surrender both worlds.
If you could smell this pain, even in another heart,
you would find release and true delight
all through your days and your nights.

182. To have provision is—
to be full of the All
then to journey empty-handed
through this nothingness.

183. Love is beyond expression.
If both worlds turn into tongues
and praise love for an eternity
nothing can be said of this affair.

184. Our Pir dropped all convention and surrendered
religion,[4]
and after a cup of love in "Deyre Moqhan," the
Magian's tower,
he declared, "I worship that rose whose thorns
carpet love's path leading the lover home,"
and then he roared, "Ana-ol Haqq[5], I am the truth"
and ascended the gallows.
In Master's footsteps Attar fell in line
and has since followed.

185. On day one
a drop of love glowed from the Unseen.
Heavenly spheres collapsed and all souls cried out,
but finding chests empty of its scent
this particle left and returned to its abode.

---

4 Here by "religion" is meant habitual acts of crowd-pleasing worship.

5 Hallaj Mansour, the Sufi saint.

186. Bu-Ali Toosi, that great lover
and beloved of God said,
"Days that are followed by nights
do not deserve this story in my heart.
To speak of this affair
one has to wait for the day
that knows not a night!"

187. You ask me who has stolen my heart.
I can't tell You it's You, I dare not,
and if I do, You will pretend You never heard,
and never give me your heart.
Attar does magic with his words to get your ear,
though you never pay heed and pretend not to hear.

188. In a besieged town preparing to fall[6]
where the populace were mourning their loss
and yesterday's lions were hiding like mice,
a lunatic ascended the highest tower
and raised his beloved King's beloved banner.
"On this day of reckoning, serve me well o' sweet lunacy,"
he said, "for I have well obliged you for a lifetime!"

[6] A town about to fall is an ancient Sufi symbol for a human body to be conquered by death.

189. Story

Haroon Al-Rashid, the great sultan,
heard Majnoon's story and wanted to see
if Leylee was indeed such a beauty.
"She is not much," he told her suitor afterwards,
"forget her, young man, resume your life!"
"Great sultan," said Majnoon unamused,
"The shortcoming is not in Leylee but in your sight,
for her ladyship won't hold court
with anyone who hasn't got what is required.
To see her undisguised
one needs Majnoon's eyes and his heart."

190. Story

In the book *Sustenance for Hearts*
that great man of the heart, Abu-Taleb Al-Makki, says,
"Every day in the Lord's all consuming light
an entire host of angels find annihilation,
and multitudes of hosts run to have their turn in
  the jubilation.
After bowing to Adam at their Lord's command,
they found a particle of love sprouting in their being,
and since then, realizing the path to the Lord runs
  through the human soul,
they have made an eternal covenant to serve humankind."

191. The Prophet has said,
"Everyday a group of angels descend
and seek a house in which God is spoken of.
There they gather and devote themselves
to being nourished by such secrets as they may hear."

192. Beloved
in the name of that heart which has never betrayed
the love you lay there in trust,
and in the name of the soul
which is never defiled
I beg You to end this separation.

193. Love is—
to unseat your clever mind
so out of a drop the sea may appear.

194. The Cupbearer handed me a cup of wine,
"Drink and be silent," I was advised.
When I had, a sun rose in my soul
and though I had been told to be silent
my soul wailed until the Beloved dropped the veil.
In my great fear and trepidation
I saw the world full of me,
though of me no trace was there.
No one can describe this,
for everyone vanishes here.

195. Our beautiful Cupbearer appeared in that joy
only youth in its first love is capable of.
"Where is the destination, what are its signs?"
asked the lover after emptying a cup.

"Where all signs vanish and all paths disappear
there you find the destination, that is our goal,"
said the Charmer of hearts.
The lover heard this and surrendered his soul.

196. I asked the Beloved about Attar's heart.
"You've lost it. You look for it," was the retort!

197. Through the secret door in my soul
Love appeared last night and roared,
"Bring me a goblet from your bleeding heart,
for I am thirsty."
My forlorn heart jumped with ecstasy and offered her all.
Love nestled in my heart and my heart rested in Love,
and there can't be, in the whole world,
a more wonderful story than that.

198. O Saqi, tonight abandon us not and grant us that wine
which erases from the heart both mine and thine.
Then let the cup drop and shatter at the preacher's door;
mayhap he will step on a piece of glass
and let a drop enter through his foot and release
his heart!

199. If you take a single breath
forgetful of this love
that breath will complain
when you come face to face with your Beloved.
Divorce both worlds and step lightly on this road.

200. "Why this suffering and pain,
this burning despair?" I asked.
"I have you here believing that you exist
to thus give you a taste
of being separated from Me," said the Beloved.

201. Love's nature is to be outside both worlds.
It is unlike anything anyone might say it is.
Love is hidden from itself.

202. One late night Leylee whispered in Majnoon's heart,
"You who for my sake have left reason behind,
listen well—
in this love your sanity you'll learn to disdain
for among lovers shrewdness brings only pain.
In the court of love if you wish to fare well
become a lunatic, throw your wits to the wind,
plunder your reason,
and from all cleverness abstain."

203. It is the soul's restless longing
that brings a human heart to life,
and a single coquettish glance from the Beloved
grants a soul its dream
after which
a lifetime of wailing is the lover's lot.

204. One who had gone mad in this fierce love,
whom lunacy had saved from his trickster self,
turned his face towards heavens and said,
"O God, You care not for me,
but I have none but You in all the worlds
and care for nothing but your love.
How do I express this, my love, my very life,
why can You not learn from me how to love?"

205. Whoever has felt a spark of this fire
appreciates the burning moans of the lunatics,
for they have surrendered their all,
and whatever they look at, to them is but a dream.
This entire world they find a mirage—
all this noise and fury, nothing but a bagpipe!

206. Before you are given a particle of this sorrow
you need to be as steady as the mountains
and as serene as a calm ocean.

207. On his way to prayers on the mountain
Moses came across a pious man who begged for blessings;
and there was one, forlorn and teary eyed,
who wanted him to ask God if He still loved him.
He then came across a love-stricken lunatic who yelled
at him,
"Look! tell Him I am at the end of my rope, I am
through burning,
I am done with You, You be done with me!"
Moses passed them all quietly.

Once with his Lord, he spoke of the two and God said,
"For the man of prayer, my blessings, and sweet love for
the other;
but what of my lunatic, why have you not mentioned
him?"
"I dared not my Lord, though you know everything,"
said Moses.

"Tell him God said," You are mine forever,
I will never leave you, whether you part or stay with me."

208. **Story**

A lover was finally summoned by his beloved
to arrive secretly and receive his heart's desire.
At his beloved's door he began to wonder
what he should say when she asks who it is.

"Should I say 'It's me,' and risk being told,
'Then go, you don't need me'?
"Or should I say, 'This too is you' . . .
and risk hearing,
'Then be gone, we have no need for you!'"

And before he could answer his questions
dawn had arrived and roosters were singing!
A sincere one who heard the story said,
"A prudent philosopher, yes,
but a lover, he wasn't."

209. To love God is—
to stop blocking your soul
so it can offer itself
to the Soul of souls.

210. Belonging to God is—
to be released from yourself,
and to find only the Friend
in your heart of hearts.

211. That ocean of light, Abol-Hasan of Kharaqhan, said,
"The heart of the one who walks in perfect poverty
is black."
And I shall tell you what he meant:
in absolute black no shadows are found.

212. The lover's soul is a wanderbird
whose sustenance is outside the two worlds.
To comprehend this mystery
you have searched heavens and earth,
it's time you spent forty days in the depth of your heart.
O'Attar, in this lane none is greater that Bu-Saeed[7]
dead to himself, alive to God.

7 Shortened version of (Sheikh) Abu Saeed Abil Kheir.

213. Steadfastness is—
to offer your soul in friendship
then to demand persistence
from every hair on your body.

214. You know your Beloved is satisfied with you
when you are satisfied with yourself.

215. Patience is—
to let the fire in you burn
and burn you to ashes,
then to die to the ashes!

216. Whatever there is, is He
and whatever is He, you are.
In reality He is all, and you never are but a reflection
you see,
and a resonance you hear.
Of your self, a single point has been shown you,
and you have become attached to it.
Let this single point circle all existence,
for that is what in truth you are.

217. From every particle there is a path to the Friend,
but none is better than surrender.
Surrender to love and you will be lifted—
the less you become, the higher you rise here.

218. Elation is—
to leave the narrowness of the two worlds
so as to experience a hundred other worlds.

219. Stop wanting to know secrets,
convert to Attar's religion—die to yourself.
Your knowing will lock this gate,
Love only comes to those
who vanish from themselves.

220. Nearness is—
to come very close to the fire,
and like a moth
to find your joy in the flame.

221. Love is to shed your self
to bow to this lunacy, and leaving your mind behind,
to reside in this nonbeing forever;
to forget both the beginning and the end,
and to dissolve in the secret of the present.

222. Last night that Beloved appeared and roared,
"Why are you not moaning,
and why is your heart not burning,
have you no shame?"
"O' my All," I begged,
"release me from myself please."
"What me is that? And aren't you ashamed of that self?"
I was thus silenced.

223. I am lost night and day
in this search for You.
You, who are never absent,
how long will I search for You?

224. I am not for a moment absent from You.
The one who is forgetful of You
is an alien residing in me.

225. Longing is—
from your shell to break out
and to dare the ocean of pain
without a raft in sight.

226. Sometimes I light up in delight,
sometimes I smolder in confusion and fright,
I am told by that Confuser of lovers,
"Don't get attached to whatever you are taught!"

227. There is a wonder in this heart,
and I am so lost in it that I can't find me.
Of the things in books, lectures and speeches,
I know enough to know that
this is neither written nor taught.

228. Come, my sleepy heart, listen,
don't be so distant.
Inside every particle it is declared,
"Here I am, come."

229. O' heart, once drunk on the wine of love,
close your mouth, don't sell God's secrets,
don't become a stream of words,
hold your tongue till you become the sea.

230. Persevere in this captivity here
though your heart suffer, for suffering refines.
A hundred colors of sorrow are offered you here
until to you they all become the same.

231. My Beloved whispered in my heart,
"Be Mine
and you will fare better than belonging to your desires.
You are self-willed out of ignorance;
become Mine and you'll have your desire."

232. Wondering if my heart is worthy of this fierce love,
I am drowned in fear one moment
and surface in hope the next.

233. In my solitude I am served this wine,
and when I am helplessly drunk
I am sent to the marketplace
and commanded to practice sobriety.
I am pulled out of this world entirely,
then sent back here with a hundred errands.

234. If you claim servanthood
then be against falsehood.
Make your home nowhere
and be eternally home.
Should servanthood pain you
let his Godhood be your delight.

235. Beloved, when he was lowered into the well
Joseph was seeking that wine
which brings nearness to You.
Mansour[8] walked up the gallows
in anticipation of union with You.
You are life's soul and whoever takes a single step in
your direction
finds felicity in both worlds.

236. If the spheres could develop vision
and see the glory of a mustard seed
they would forever be bewildered.
The spheres, the mustard seed and all else in both worlds
are but particles on the Beloved's garment.

[8] Hallaj Mansour: the Sufi saint.

237. As life's secrets and wonders
my Beauty is laid out here as a gift to the seeing eye,
though the blind will never come to see
and always speak of the hidden jewel.

238. The cure for this pain of longing is yet more longing.
Lovers drink a thousand oceans
and still burn with thirst.
When Attar is completely erased of himself
a tiny particle of his soul contains the nine spheres.

239. If an ant knocks at Your door it is not ignored.
And that's how merciful You are.
I am only capable of weakness and sin. And that's how wretched I am.
Where can I take refuge
if I am driven away from Your door?

240. I left miracles and stations of power behind
and found my way to the wine shop in the Magi's tavern.
I followed the drunken libertines and gave up
crowd pleasing, idle talk and pretending.
Once I lost my cleverness to the wine of love,
with other mad lovers I began this litany.

241. Abu Saeed Abil-kheir,
that all-knowing bird[9], said,
"For thirty years I sought It,
when I found what I was looking for, I vanished in It.
Now how can someone who is lost
find that which he has lost?"

242. The other day
I found myself in the strangest state—
one instant I was clearly dead
the next moment I was having a new birth.
Now I can only wail and wail some more
because for a moment I remembered that
which now I can remember not.

---

[9] Reference is to Attar's masterpiece, *Manteq-al-tair (The Conference of the Birds)* in which the main character leads other birds in their quest for truth.

243. This madness granted me
can never be tamed;
they tell me to come down to earth!
Might as well put the ocean in chains!

244. This is a most baffling affair,
one of the two has to be true—
either I am not,
or there is nothing other than me.

245. You are my purpose
and your abode is my destination;
no fear if I lose heart, mind and soul,
that is what they are all for!

246. I knocked on this door for a lifetime
arguing hows and whys
and dreaming insanity.
When it was opened,
I realized I'd been knocking from inside.

247. To look at a particle
and behold in it all Infinity
is an awesome sight;
when the Beloved revealed this to my soul
I moaned, "What should I do?"
"What *can* you do?"
was the coquettish retort.

248. In my solitude last night
I came upon Deyr-e Moqhan,
the hermitage of the magi
where Pir-e Moqhan, the Master,
who, drunk on love's sacred wine,
from himself had been released,
offered me a cup.
After I drank from his hands
every particle in creation revealed its message:
"The Friend is the Beloved and the Lover too.
The rest, stage props and a great ado."

249. Sometimes, after my laments at dawn
I receive a gift from You.
Sometimes, after my sighs burn me through
I feel You.
But more than anything, I delight in my own absence
in that Presence where there's only You.

250. Beloved,
one who does not in this life
find joy in that sweet sorrow
which is missing You
will find only death here,
and be covered under a pile of dirt.

251. You find your Beloved where you lose yourself.

252. The Friend is ever with us
both within and without,
and yet everyone is seeking after Him.
Standing on the shore of the sweetest ocean
we are all parched, dying of thirst.
Be ever patient with this affliction Attar,
the Friend decides the when and the how.

253. Beloved, I have no one and nowhere to turn—
a lowly beggar at your door, a worn out bag of bones,
my heart is drowning in its tears and my soul is on fire.
I am a nobody who happens to know a Friend of Yours.
Beloved, I died here before I died;
in this secret please be my help and my guide.
You are the maker and keeper of all there is;
pray release this particle and let it vanish,
for I was not meant to remain,
but You are eternal and so You shall remain.

254. To live in your Beloved's command is—
to find your soul in servanthood
and to let every particle of you
be annihilated in the Beloved's wish.

255. Someone asked Majnoon
in which direction to pray.
"Majnoon's Kabaa is Leylee's face,
for lovers pray in the direction the Beloved rests,
otherwise pray in the direction of a stone structure
which forever has a human soul for its own
prayer direction,"
he said.
Where the soul is granted intimacy in the inner sanctum
a hundred thousand confounded Kabaas flutter in
bewilderment.

256. Whatever you may know about the mystery of God
you have read it in the pages
of your book of illusions.
You can learn about the Friend only through the Friend;
when you die to all qualities
you vanish in his essence.

257. The Beloved said,
"If I wish, in an instant I'll create two worlds
in a particle's heart,
if not I'll shut my door
and gone will be stars and humans."
Realize o' dear one
it is the absolutely needless One
who is having this play with your soul.

258. No tears change that which has been ordained.
If both worlds vanish at this moment,
to the Almighty it is neither a gain nor a loss.

258.1 Beloved
out of your infinite mercy fulfill my heart's desire;
let your "Huzur," your Presence, ever be my shelter;
save me from myself and make me an intimate;
and when my last breath draws near let me breathe with
You, free of fear.

259. The real calamity is that
we are all afloat in this ocean
and entirely oblivious of it.

260. If your Beloved graces you
but a thousand enemies surround you, worry not.
If you have beheld your Beloved
don't fret about being stoned to death.
If you are Mansour[10] and you can declare yourself
the Truth,
then surrender to the gallows and worry not.

261. Beloved, if someday you drop the veil
people will behold You and declare
I too am the Truth!

262. Whoever drinks a drop from this ocean,
from both worlds he wants to be erased.
A single breath in this Presence is all life is worth.
Become an intimate and surrender heaven and earth,
for one is made of steam, the other of dirt.

---

10 Hillaj Mansour, the Sufi saint.

263. Every dawn I go to my Beloved,
yet from myself I keep it a secret.
Attar, how long this degradation in your company?

264. When I beheld my Beloved's beauty
my eyes turned towards heaven and I lost my tongue.
I lost myself and I have no idea where—
a drop vanished in the sea, a shadow vanished in the sun.
In this Affair one needs to be schooled in complexities
without losing one's simplicity,
one needs to shut one's eyes before one can see.

265. My Beloved's guile is confounding.
I am rejected in all appearance,
but lifted and embraced within.
A bitter word from that Beloved is all Attar can hope for,
and for that his soul he will happily offer.

266. Every moment the Beloved is differently beautiful—
that's why every moment
Farid[11] comes up with a different song of praise.

267. I journey through this world in confusion.
In both worlds I have none other than the Friend,
and of him, nowhere can I find a trace.

268. Last night the Friend said,
"Though we visit only now and then
wherever you go you are with Me,
and for your every step towards Me
I cover both worlds to come to you.
Why not abandon yourself
since separation from Me
is not in your destiny?"

11 Farid: one of Attar's pen names.

269. At night
when the sun of my soul rises
and my Beloved arrives,
I think of a thousand tricks
to stitch my night to eternity
wishing the day would never arrive.

270. My Beloved said last night,
"You have become a stranger,
is that how one behaves?
You have deserted your Friend
is that how it should be?
You've been away from Me a couple of days
and are acting like a stranger.
Is that how in separation a lover behaves?"

271. Beloved, hidden or revealed
there is none but You,
though knowledge and intellect
find not their way to You.
Pray, open a window into my shuttered heart,
so I can sit there and lose myself in the view.

272. When you behold your heart and see no darkness
you will see a drop from that ocean that is the Beloved.
Then in the center of unity in your soul
you will find the circle of infinity.

273. The Friend holds all existence
like a mirror in his hands
and beholds his own countenance.
In the sounds of existence in the worlds
He hears his own praise.

274. One thing
which is not a thing
and can't be numbered
is All there is.
And It is the Darling of Creation,
whatever the soul decrees
It is that,
and It is beyond all decrees!

275. Beloved, You granted me a taste of this Affair,
and put in my heart this flair.
That's what has brought me here,
and the same will guide me back There.
If every hair on my body turns into a tongue
it will utter nothing other than Your name.
And should a single particle of me remain and
nothing else
it will sing of You and adore You and none else.

276. Beyond belief and disbelief
is this friendship with You;
beyond beginning and end
is this relationship.

277. How strange
one never reaches You
while one is never without You
nor can ever leave You.

278. Beloved
You are covered with veils
and I am full of illusions;
the journey is far
and no one can guess in which direction.

279. Though I can't see You
I see the world full of You.
You wanted your lover to cry—
to become invisible You hid in his eye.

280. I am bewildered in this thought day and night
that You are ever with me but I am ever lost.
You are the sweetest ocean and yet,
stricken by the fear of the waves
I am standing on the shore, wasting away in my thirst.

281. This world and the next are veils,
and You have withdrawn and reside in silence.
You tell me to search for You in my soul,
but how can I find my way to my soul?

282. All that is
is You.
Who then is this, searching for You?

283. What talisman ensnares us
that we are with You
but live this separation?
Since You are all and the rest is null,
why are we nothings still here?
Erase our hearts from all else
so, like Farid[12], we become singular
and singularly belong to You.

[12] Farid: one of Attar's pen names.

284. The whole world is beauty and songs,
but when one is deaf and blind what can be done?
Beloved, You sit within and outside there is no one;
pull me within so I may be an intimate.
One who has You, what need does he have of anyone?

285. The world is full of You,
but in my ignorance I am absent from You.
You are here and present;
it is my presence that is lacking!

286. You who reside in the traceless absolute,
who do I ask for my way to You?
You who reside inside my soul,
where do I look for a sign of You?

287. All I want from You Beloved
is for all my wants to vanish.
In the realm of surrender there's no despair
even if the two worlds, and all of us in them, were
to disappear.

288. Destiny has put this longing for You in my heart,
and yet You are thoroughly needless of me.
I have no one I can turn to,
neither do I have the patience for this separation.

289. Hallaj became "Mansoor," the victorious,
because he found a thousand thrones
when, in Your name, he dared the gallows.
Attar chose nonexistence after he realized
by being mired in existence he is distanced from You.

290. Every particle in creation
turns to You in adoration;
every human in prayers faces in your direction.
Whether they know it or not,
creatures in both worlds
eternally long to return to your fold.
In truth, none other than You can ever be loved,
it's only in remembrance of You that others are loved.

290.1 Whoever fails to find joy
in his longing for You
well deserves the pile of dirt bestowed upon him
when this world is done and finished with him.

291. Though You fill the seven skies
no one can have enough of You
or hear enough about You.
My heart's Life,
how can You leave me so empty-handed
when the whole world is so totally filled by You?

292. You, in whose love the soul blossoms
please hear my plea:
If this lonely affair
this lunatic is granted the strength to bear,
I'll someday be the king of every sphere.

292.1 Beloved, glorious is that single-pointed devotion
which brings the love You trusted in our hearts
in pre-eternity
back to You without any omission.
Glorious is that intimacy granted by You
where archangel Gabriel dares not to interfere.

293. Our togetherness no one detects,
our tongue no one can decipher.
You are with me eternally,
what then is this separation I suffer?

294. I have neither what it takes
to be with You
nor the desire to take a single breath
away from You.
My sighs will surely burn this world down
if I remain here without You.

295. When I lose my mind
You hear my story,
when I lose my hearing
I hear your response.

296. Since You made your appearance in my heart
both worlds have disappeared from it,
and my heart has vanished in You.

297. Longing for You for even a breath
is more precious than the two worlds.
No tongue may praise you properly—
that only You can do.

297.1 For the one who can hear
let a single piece of advice suffice—
never take a breath without the Beloved,
watch your breaths and you will be raised high.
Enough of words, let's taste silence now;
enough of poems, let's take refuge in their Bestower.

298. Annihilation is—
to surrender the self to arrive at nonself,
then to take leave of both.

299. Aloof You are from everyone
yet You are with everyone.
When I become silent like a sealed letter
You take over as the reader of sealed letters.

300. Whatever has a name and is in creation
is but a dewdrop from that ocean—
this you realize when you have left behind
that which is called one's mind.
For though it helps one's start,
once the soul awakes mind can only be left behind—
since one's soul is a heavenly bird,
and compared to that mind's but a dead horse.

300.1 A lover said, "I asked God for three things—
a swift death in sleep,
an eternal rest in death,
and as for the third, what can one say?
For it cannot be said!

301. Beloved, make me absent from myself
and never let me go back;
for if I be a dog at your gate, without me
fortune itself will envy my infinite luck.

302. Die once, before your body dies,
and death will bring you an eternal gift.

303. One who sinks in this sorrow that is your love
has no worries in either world.
If Attar is left without this pain
his heart will be empty of joy, and his soul empty of life.

304. I suffered until I surrendered heart and soul
and became an emperor.
Now, released from that curse that was me,
I and my Beloved live within the same shirt.

305. I have become lost to myself
and will never go back to it.
In this Affair Attar can only be a veil;
I'll never again seek his company.

306. I drank from this wine at dawn
which, opening a trapdoor in my heart,
let the stream flowing there enter the ocean.
There, I drowned and all conventions died with me,
and now I am neither living nor dead,
and this none can understand.
A perilous place you have landed yourself, Attar;
it's all up to you now, for I have been spared!

307. You can't journey There
if yourself you do not abandon,
for one who does so, in an instant achieves
that which takes lifetimes here.

308. Spread the prayer mat of surrender
and sit still.
In a house made of flesh and bones one cannot keep a dog.
Evict the dog of your ego
and be still.

308.1 Equity is—
to bring fairness into all your affairs
while expecting it from no one else.

309. I would die joyfully
if while living I could die for a moment and thus
live like a human is meant to live.

310. I died before the angel of death paid a visit
and realized my pure essence.
Now I am not afraid of surrendering the flesh—
for that skin, I have already shed.

311. Nothing is more certain than death
and yet, ponder this great wonder
that no one ever considers death!

312. The day I died to my existence
in my drunken needlessness I covered that distance
which otherwise burns a thousand savants to ashes.

313. To find the Essence is—
to become a mirror to thyself,
then to appear in front of it.

314. When the soul vanishes in light
it enters the heaven of the pure ones.
One who is thus clad in divinity
is a message from God to himself.
You who have been blessed within and without
step forward then and receive this gift of light.

315. Since your Lord is always with you
walk and act in this Presence;
for every step you take in denial
brings you only remorse and betrayal.

316. Entertain only those thoughts
which if they were to surface and be seen by the world
would bring you no shame.
Live in this world such that if the angel of death were to appear this moment
hesitation would not assail your heart.

316.1 This world fattens you for slaughter and this,
you should understand, is not by intent but by its nature.
No matter who you are and what you do,
at the end, life will have her way with you.

317. Should you desire union
your very soul you should surrender.
When you reach where you should
you weigh your mind against your soul.
Should it weigh more, you tarry yet awhile,
but should your soul find herself unburdened with
your mind
then it melts into the soul of souls.

317.1 Vice is—
to be waylaid by filth
and to mix musk with the stench of disobedience.

318. Sobriety is—
to find a way through yourself
and learn about the One,
then to discard your self.

319. **U**nion is—
to step from existence into life,
then to abandon both
to taste the bliss of being.

320. **R**apture is—
to drown in the joy of the true dawn
and to be aflame in the absence of the sun.

321. **S**tory

The veils were dropped one night
and the great Sheikh of Kharaqhan begged,
holding his Beloved in clear sight,
"For sixty years I've been looking for You,
my Lord. Erase me from myself
and let me be this light."
"My own dear Abol-Hasan," said the Lord,
"that seeking which arose in your soul
did not appear of its own accord,
it was My desire for you that pulled you."
When you realize that the One you want
is the One who fills your soul with desire,
you find yourself alive without your self
and become an eternal guiding light.

322. Story

A lunatic in Neyshaboor told me once,
when of his dereliction and madness I asked,
"I witnessed the sun rise one day and enter my chest,
myself and both worlds in that fire I lost."

They asked him how he felt when he was dying.
"How could you even begin to know?" he said,
  and passed.

323. Story

Nizam the great vizir once saw a perfect one on the road.
"Ask me for something," said the great minister,
"and I will oblige with delight."
"I have quit asking, even from God,
I surely have no need of you," said he.
"Then accept a request from a fallen one.
When you are with God, just remember me once,
and all my worries will be put to rest."
"Here's a complete dunce for you," said the sky clad.
"When that boon is given me, I'm made absent
  from myself.
How can I take someone there where I myself am lost?"

324. A heathen or a believer it matters not.
Be a drop, then, whether you are a wise one or a lunatic,
to the ocean how can it matter?

325. A perfect one was once asked
what his wish for the hereafter was,
and this was his reply:
"Released from the vagaries of a wayward eye,
and that scatteredness which is this mind,
there'll be my soul and her Beloved, the Lord,
with no veils in between,
and for all eternity
she will stare at her Beloved's beauty."

325.1 Ecstasy is—
to step beyond dogmas and your beliefs both,
and to learn the inner truth.

326. The day my heart became an intimate to this Mystery
it heard a thousand melodies inside.
For thirty years my heart had run after thoughts,
now it had to return and confess to its follies.

327. Gratitude is—
to see a thorn and to consider it a rose,
to see a fragment
and be mindful of the whole.

328. You study the candle for a lifetime
and describe and analyze its light,
and what great good it has done you.
All you had to do was ask the moth.

329. O' slumbering ones,
a hundred stations beyond wisdom I'll travel
and finally be released from good and evil.
There, I will meet beauty, the unveiled me,
and fall in love with my self.

330. The other night
I heard the moth tell the candle,
"Be mine tonight."
"Only if you step into the flame
and burn bright," said the candle.

331. In its love for the candle
the moth finds its salvation;
it dances and flutters around the flame
till it turns to ashes and steps outside the prison of
its body.

332. When I am allowed behind the veil of mysteries,
I become a doer in both worlds.
They say no one returns from the other world,
yet I do so every day, and some days more than once!

333. "I am a tiny drop," the heart lamented;
"how can I ever have the ocean's company?"
But when it finally fell in the ocean and drowned
it screamed, "This ocean is me."

333.1 My heart is bloodied in this abode of fears;
only a heart of stone doesn't bleed here.

334. A drop can find the ocean only as wide as its
own vision.
Where the vision is limited, there the drop imagines
a shore,
for how else could the drop see a shore to this
shoreless ocean?

335. The soul that is granted the center
sees as one, past, present and future,
and the beginning and eternity as the same.
O' darveesh[13], why all this talk of return
when we've never left?

336. If the inner reality of all
is the Beloved
what could the outer reflection be
other than the Beloved?

---

13 Darveesh: literally a poor one, in Sufi lore it denotes a true practitioner/seeker.

337. To Gain is—
to learn from the candle to abandon oneself to the flame
while bringing light to the world.

338. I heard the burning moth scream,
"I am on fire, my end is here."
"So it is," said the candle,
"a moment more and you are released,
but I am to burn yet, to light up the night."

339. A thirsty bird who had heard of the ocean
found its way there after struggling a lifetime.
"Now every drop is mine," it said, and
after the first sip it fell in and died.

340. The river boiling with power
faces obstacles and fights
till it reaches the ocean, and there
it rests as if it had forever been motionless.

341. In the secret pages of the alchemy of union I read
that nonexistence is the essence of true faith.
If you don't want to remain locked out and perish
in front of the gate to your true self,
this you remember should you forget all else.

342. Whoever seeks You on his own
gets stranded in eternal separation,
but whoever you grant a moment in union,
in both worlds only that moment he considers life.

343. You who read these words
look deeply and realize
the absence of verbal trickery.
A poet, call me not, I am not that,
for I am a man of the present
not of the poets past.

344. Since the eye of my soul beheld the truth
many gems have surfaced in my heart.
Your poetry paints the soul in words Attar,
wherefore it bewilders some minds!

345. To write poetry is
to uncover love's story
and great wonders to describe;
but though here secrets be given free flight
it may not be prudent to carry on too long,
since anyone who has pondered along thus far,
for the rest has been granted the foresight.

346. When the wayfarer finds the soul's secret
he comes to life, and being worthy of servanthood
faces the Creator in that delight
where in each breath a hundred lives' joys reside.

The soul's journey in truth commences only then,
but were I to divulge here even a few words
it would surely unravel the two worlds.

Yet, were I to be granted another life,
and were the command to come from above,
my soul would not shirk from its duty
and I would tell you of this grand Affair
in a new book to illumine both here and hereafter.
But of this present journey enough has been given you—
tarry no longer therefore and may God be with you.

347. Lord, please allow me to be summoned
when I am drowned in prayers
my face awash in my tears
and my forehead carrying the dust
with which it was graced
touching the ground at your behest.

348. I was a bird come here from the unseen;
I sojourned here for a spate and now take my leave.

349. Dear ones, I have recounted a lover's story
and now from the solitude of your heart
I beg for blessings and prayers for my hour of need,
for only God can truly be needless.

350. Lord, in light bathe those
who, after reading these lines, find it in their hearts
to remember me in their prayers and thoughts.

A lot has been said and from speech
in silence have we arrived.

EPILOGUE

There is a tradition in the Middle-East of asking for blessings from those one may feel an especial affinity with. It is in this spirit that Attar asks for the blessings of his readers in the concluding pages of almost every book he pens.

Noble Sirs
Should a line here speak to your heart
send this poor one a blessing thought,
for unto a dark grave it may shed some light,
and an allotted punishment may thus be forgot.
And though to your noble self it has been no pain
your soul, through this blessing, may stand to gain.

—Farideddin Attar Neyshaboori

May the Sheikh be brought closer and closer to his Beloved, and ours, and may his soul be bathed in Light.

APPENDIX

Moseebat-nameh (*The Book of Travails*) is an allegorical story in 7425 lines of verse about the journey of remembrance for the soul which, smothered by the mind, has forgotten its Essence and Origin.

Around this main thread are woven a large number of stories often based on some well known mystics' lives and teachings.

Under the guidance of his Master, the Pir, the seeker (the questioning mind!) embarks on a journey during which he has meetings and exchanges with a number of Prophets, angels, and even elemental forces, and begs for help only to be reminded that they cannot do it for him and that he needs to do the work himself. He always brings his experiences to his Pir who advises him and provides guidance for further progress on the Path.

Here you will find an abridged account of a few of the encounters which Attar masterfully brings together throughout *Moseebat-nameh*, a journey of spiritual awakening, and the final merging of the individuated consciousness into Consciousness, the drop in The Ocean.

The Soul's Journey

1. With coverings do away and listen well if you may.
Whether these poems speak of firmaments,
atoms, people, angels and Prophets
remember, they are from inner experience and not hearsay.
Call them revelations if you wish
and let's proceed.

2. In triple darkness
from a blood clot and supreme waters
the fetus appears.
When ready, upon it a Light shines.
Of this body one may speak,
but of this Light
it is useless to talk.

3. That to which angels in a hundred worlds
were ordered by God to bow to
is not of water and dirt,
but of soul, a Divine secret.
Is there a wish in your heart
to explore how a handful of dirt may turn into pure soul?

4. If you are not granted this pain
how could you dream of a cure?
If you care not to be called a servant,
how could you hope to be summoned?

If your own pain and fame you won't let go
in this flame you will not glow.

5. For a fetus to thirst for soul
it must journey through that sorrow
whose cure is yet more sorrow.
The journey to that station is long and arduous,
but once there, eternal ecstasy and joy is yours.

6. That longing which overtakes the seeker
is the treasure all creation is after.

The story of the soul's trials and triumphs
is the story of this book;
heed well if you be interested.

7. What in dreams are oft witnessed
should not be rejected if to some
they be revealed in wakefulness;
for though some visions be of demonic design
others are truths angelic and Divine.
Discernment and steadfast love are needed here
to separate the holy from the profane.

8. The seeker rushes to find that alchemy
which will manifest soul from body
soon to blow away in the dust.

One reflects, ponders, and ponders more,
for this can be done in no other way,
and as those who have will tell you:
an hour of true reflection here brings you closer
than seventy years of prayers may.

9. Wit and efforts are but a doorknob
on the Beloved's door.
Without the Master's grace
the doorknob never turns
and one finds no solace.

10. Here one can find no one truly sincere
in his beliefs or in his affairs,
no contact with those who have passed on,
and no comfort from the stories they left behind.
In this fierce confusion
a true one standing on true feet
is truly rare and finding him is great fortune.

11. In this blizzard of confusion raging here
everyone comes to pillage or to crave.
Under a pile of gold a slinking pauper hides,
behind a pretty face a scorpion resides.
One bedecks his beard in diamonds and rubies,
the first chance he gets he licks a bowl of grease.
The school master is mired in his own lies,
the preacher, looks serious, but is an entertainer
in disguise.
The upright leaves the stage to the misbegotten,
swift hawks here become beasts of burden.

12. Those ruled here by their heart
can't wait for the day to come to night;
they face the wall and ponder their captivity
while everyone else, trapped deep in the bottom of
his well,
is busy interpreting the entire universe.

13. A thousand lusts with a thousand ills in their tow
besiege the mind here, high and low.
Numberless whirlpools appear churning the ocean,
every particle there seeking its own salvation.
Wandering away from his wit and senses
the confounded seeker sifts the dirt a thousand times,
only a thousand useless stones to find.

14. Perilous and long is the journey,
and we are like unto the blind.
Should you attempt this without a guide
you will, if yourself be a lion, fall in a well and be
left behind.

15. The Lord, taking pity on the wanderer,
finally comes to his aid.
And the one whose I-ness is vanished
and is united with the Lord appears in his life.

16. Every step and every stop of the way
the Master has completed.
In this place, but from the placeless,
with his times, but of the timeless,

the Knower of the secret of every atom—
He is the One who is bewitched by no object.

17. Though from the public they may be hidden
Masters know the world's condition.
Despair not if you do not find your Pir fast,
for without one, time and place would not exist.
Once you are granted this thirst
you shall be guided to his throne,
for he is crowned and anointed by the Beloved
to anoint wounded hearts and attend to our fate.

18. When the seeker is finally brought to a living Pir,
his radiance lights up his soul
and, set afire, it begins to stir;
light appears and darkness flees.

Love chases cleverness and greed away
a thousand flowers of unspeakable beauty
appear and blossom in the seeker's heart.

Like a spring thunderstorm, tears rain—
he cries and laughs as his soul lifts.
These he well knows he has not earned,
but come from the Pir as blessings and gifts.

Sunk in the bosom of the ocean, from a drop of rain
many years of toil may bring forth a pearl—
such is the story of a pilgrim soul and its sacred tale.

19. When the seeker is prepared
he is put on the Path and told,
"Long is the journey, many the hurdles
with robbers behind many an obstacle.
Strive and be not attached, not even to a particle;
for if you be snagged anywhere on this road
there you shall end up and suffer for good.
Walk straight, face bitterness and carry your load;
pay heed to the longing in your heart, let that be
your guide."

20. The seeker surrenders to his longing
and gives up his complaints and demanding;
and stepping onto the infinite path
does a hundred hells and heavens find.
When he tarries he is summoned in fierce rush,
when he rushes he is but sent away.
Many doors he knocks on only to be turned down,
many times he dreams of flying
only to realize it is not yet his time.
He finds himself in a hundred crooked tunnels—
the more he seeks the less he finds.
Bewildered, he sees himself a travelling merchant
whose beast of burden is dead—
his goods are scattered,
his destination is far, and no road signs are to be found.
He finally loses his cares and, stumbling upon
sweet lunacy,
he surrenders his cleverness
and is granted intimacy.
Only then does he witness his drunken flight in ecstasy.

21. O' Beloved, my pain and my cure
the Soul of my soul, my belief and my disbelief as well
if You make me carry a thousand mountains
You are the doer, who am I to make such boasts?
I know nothing about You,
but You are this most wonderful longing,
and should I lose my soul to You, I will have gained it all.

22. If I cry, I am told not to carry on;
if I laugh, I am ordered to cry.
If I sleep not, You command sleep;
if I do, I am told not to,
and then I am asked why not.
One never knows what to do with You.
Begging You is not a vice nor a virtue,
one can call You neither a foe nor a friend!

23. Leily was told Majnoon was roaming the desert
sleeping under thorn bushes, out of his senses.
"What business does my lover have with roaming
or sleeping?"
said the irate beloved.
Later, whether standing, sitting, dreaming or praying
from Majnoon, "Leily" was all that could be heard.
"Now he can be trusted with his claim,
absent from himself, nothing in his life but my name,"
said the blushing beloved, and lifted the blame.

24. The seeker came to Gabriel the messenger,
"O carrier of the Qor'an, Psalms of David and the Torah,
spirit of holiness, Lord's trusted one,
I am downtrodden and lost in this pain,
I have taken refuge at your gate, pray help this fallen one."

"I am all that and then some," said Gabriel.
"Though I only carry his command and that only with
his grace,
I live in eternal awe of my Lord,
and have yet to bring myself to mention his name.
Should I ever come nearer to that domain than allowed,
tracelessly shall I vanish in that flame.
Be gone human for I can hardly bear
the weight of my own burden."

25. The dejected seeker brought his tears to his Pir.
"Gabriel is the spirit," He said, "carrier of the
Lord's command.
Seventy thousand years in obedient penance
before he had the courage to contemplate His grace.
Prior to that he stayed put, nothing but silence,
many lives on the Path just to gain the forbearance
to become worthy of the treasure of remembrance,
the highest prize any soul could ever wish for.
And what do you fancy yourself capable of, puny human?
Yet, proudly will you take his name in vain."

26. The seeker to Seraphiel appealed now,
"You who are allowed to bring life and to take,
grant me Life or let me embrace death," he said.
"I can smash this world and the next like two glass jars,
yet, I can't but fear and ponder my own plight,
and unable to contain the dread, I flee in fright.
Leave me be and go on your way,
and I will weep in my solitude both for the night and
the day,"
said Seraphiel.

The seeker brought the Pir his dilemma and heard,
"Seraphiel the pure, of creation and destruction is the sire,
no angel can fathom his grandeur; yet at the throne,
like a tiny bird in awe, he shakes every hour.
Should you too desire even a drop of such adoration
you should choose surrender and be purified in its fire."

27. "Facing this awe on the Path is not an easy affair—
a hundred worlds full of bleeding hearts parade there.
Those at a distance are spared the flames,
the closer one comes, the more bewildered one gets.
Whoever He favors is sure to drown in his own
bleeding heart,
whoever the Beloved grants calamity
is sure to taste the coming bounty.
Fly headfirst into this ocean, and should you desire favors,
be broken and tame, surrender to his orders."

28. The seeker approached Mikael,
"O keeper of all wealth without whom there can't be
any gain,
clouds rain by your command;
from the babes at their mother's breasts
to our universe, and all else are but your guests.
A forlorn child am I and much less,
pray help this lost one."

29. Mikael listened with a heavy heart, and said,
"Rain and snow are my tears, and mists my frozen sighs,
night and day, east and west, I attend to, and find no rest.
Thus I am kept from my Beloved, from my Love True.
If I be so confined and helpless
what could I do for others?
The door you search for is within your heart,
and my reach cannot extend that far."

30. The seeker again sought the Pir's company
presented his case and Mikael's litany.
"Mikael is the agent through whom
the Lord grants everyone his due,
no more than that can he be expected to do,"
said the Perfect One.

31. All and everything comes through the Giver,
here, beg for his generosity and his favor,
and within your heart search for his mystery,
and know that if you understand
that the source of all that is is There,
then There you will find your home
once you are through with your affairs here.

32. A Perfect One has said
that on this path there are an infinite number of
heartaches,
each more tantalizing than the other,
but the courage to face this Affair one cannot muster,
so behind veils he hides to spare himself its lustre.

The wine of the Beloved's favor is served
on the other shore of the desert of his severity.
Without this—that won't be secured
without heartache and pain—how can one search for
a cure?

33. The seeker now dragged himself to Azrael's door
and said, "O glorious Angel of Death, slayer of
soul's slavery,
you, whom the soul longs to see
though the body shivers in dread and calls it a folly.
While people may say he is dead and gone
you bring the soul to its Beloved and cut the separation
short; well done.
Being trapped in the body is not for the soul,
pray, release my heart from this prison
and free it from this drudgery."

34. When Azrael heard the seeker's plea
he lost his humor, you'd think he'd seen death's glee!
"Were you aware remotely of my pain and misery," said he,
"you would never come to me with your childish prattle.
A hundred thousand eons have I been assigned
to take lives from young and old alike;
a hundred worlds' blood is on my hands,
has anyone else been dealt such a foul hand?
Of my dread, if you were to hear the smallest part
you would scatter into a hundred pieces no doubt.
In your own predicament is contained your cure,
that is where you'll find your answer.
Be gone now and tarry here no more."

35. To the Master ran the seeker in dread
and told him of his encounter with the Lord of Death.
He said, "Azrael is just and spares no one.
When one dies we say he may rest now in peace.
Here, comfort comes only in death, a miserable world
is this;
but death's message comes in its own due time,
hurrying there before one's time won't do the trick.
Come, let us ascend to heavens higher above while we can
before this container of flesh and blood scatters to
the winds."

36. The seeker found his way to heaven and to angelic hosts
he said,
"All commands you deliver and all heavens you carry on
your backs,
would you not help me with my load,
for the day is late and all my companions have left,
and I have not what it takes to go forward, nor to
go back."

37. The heavenly host in unison declared:
"We are given heavens to uphold,
and though under our feet only thin air we find,
in such predicament and in constant fear
our only reason for being is to serve humankind.
Yet, your search is for the Divine love's alchemy,
and that is a quality granted humans only.
Waste not your time, you won't find it here,
for that is not something we are able to bear."

38. The Pir said, after hearing the seeker's story,
"Angels witness the glory and stand in obedience,
but in their Lord's love they do not last,
for in that fire they vanish and surrender their
very existence."

39. The key to both worlds
is a drop of the essence of human heart,
for whose fragrance angelic hosts clamor day and night.
We are swimmers in the sweetest oceans, and yet
everyone is always burning of thirst and most
die parched.

40. The seeker sought his answers in Paradise,
but here too he was told to think twice,
"For those in here are only seduced by heavenly streams
of milk and wine, honey and ambrosia.
But one with true love in his heart has no use for
such items,
as only babes and drunkards are fooled by such promises."

41. Once the seeker was at the Master's feet he heard,
"Paradise is where the ever blazing sun glows.
Whoever is warmed by that sun while still living,
from its reflection his whole being is illumined.
Whatever is promised you in heaven
look diligently and you will find it here, within your
own heart."

42. The seeker brought his case to Satan and said:
"You who first were the closest and now the farthest,
your seven hundred years of delving into secrets was of
no help
when the time came for you to be cursed.
The believer's heart you chew, and in his very blood you
spit poison,
and from east to west and north to south you were
given domain.
If you know the secret passage to my treasure
reveal it to me and you'll have cured my pain."

43. Satan was set aflame with these words and said,
"An angel for thousands of years, now I am the devil.
I am made but of regrets and you'd do well to heed,
for you are ignoring oceans of mercy on damnation
to feed.
What you will find here, you don't have the stomach for—
be hastily gone now and trouble me no more."

44. Seeing the seeker in such a fright, Master said,
"Satan is made of jealousy and of me and mine,
he is jealous of anyone courting God, and guards his gate;
and though he was cursed and sent away by the Lord,
he has eyes for no one else,
and is the ever-watchful protector of the Beloved's abode."

45. The seeker brought his case to Adam and said,
"You, who house in your chest the Lord's breath,
you, whose soul is the Imperial Bird,
you, to whom all angels had to bow at birth,
this creation was made for you and yours.
Surrendering the eight heavens
you became you to people the earth.
My heart is on fire, take pity and help me with my plight."

46. Adam said, "Though I know the secret, it'd be improper—
for the proper way is to find your own way to the Gate,
to the Prophet (PBUH),[1] under whose banner
his saints and their charge are guided home."
The seeker again took his laments to his Pir, his Master.

47. Master said, "Adam is the original principle.
He surrendered the throne of lordship to seek servanthood!
Though in himself he housed the light of sanctity
leaving joys of heaven, he lovingly chose our depravity,
and finding love in obedience, became the beloved servant."

---

[1] PBUH—Peace Be Upon Him.

48. Story

A companion complained to Hazrat Ali about life and
the world,
"This world is like unto a farm," said the Prophet's
nephew, "and tomorrow
you will eat that which you plant today.
If you die with no provisions, you'll face deep sorrow
and have no recourse on a long and difficult journey.
No idler ever sees the face of our Beloved;
this world then is the best place to work your way There."

49. The seeker approached Moses in despair and said,
"You found the highest treasure
in the middle of the night and became a king.
No shepherd has found such fortune day or night.
You are the beloved of the Emperor, pray hear
my lament—
grant me a particle of your fortune and end my torment."
"You need to become the burning bush,
for otherwise you'll never make it there.
Now leave and peace be with you," said Moses, God's
own friend.

50. Master told the seeker, when he finally made it there,
"Moses's soul is an ocean of love, among lovers he is
a senior.
Love is the treasure-house of both worlds;
whoever has claims in this Affair,
the least he has do is to offer his very soul."

51. The seeker brought his tears to David and said,
"A hundred worlds of love were brought together
placed in one soul and given the name David.
Your psalms sing of that love and the world listens.
I am lost, a particle of that fire send with me,
so I may find my way in this dark maze here."

52. "No great one ever achieved anything
without struggling with one's self for one's spirit.
Everyone who enters this path
has come to do just that.
Should you desire an audience in that court
begin your journey and present your effort,"
said David, the singer of the psalms.

53. The seeker came to the Prophet (PBUH) and said,
"You who are the purpose of creation, God's
special messenger,
I have knocked on so many doors,
helpless I have come to your door.
Ignore my shortcomings and grant me a gift—
shed light on this poor one's soul."

"As long as you are with your self, no hope,"
said the Prophet, "for your heart can't love
and your soul won't awake.
Leave sensuality and desires,
then your mind and then your heart
become a shadow; then let that shadow burn in that sun
that is your Lord's light.

Let there be nothing left of you, and God knows best.
Your road passes through five stations within:
first your self, your senses and all their dreams,
then your mind and intellect,
a place of arguments, of hair splitting;
then your heart and finally your soul—
a long, arduous road where you pay many a toll.

Once released from the five,
your self you realize and to the Self
you offer it in great gratitude.
Then you behold your Self without yourself.
Your speech then won't be your speech
though your tongue will speak it;
you will hear all there is to hear
though your hearing you will have relinquished;
and you will live, though your life you will
    have surrendered.
Once you reach there
issues of the world and of religion
will both be obvious and clear,
the mysteries you will behold there
you can't describe in a hundred thousand years.
Now then, be on your way and begin your journey."

54. When the seeker sought his Pir's counsel He said,
"The Prophet, in perfect poverty, is in the Beloved's
    company.
Whatever is given to everyone in all the worlds
is due to the souls of such poor ones,
though they may still watch every single appetite day
    and night
for fear of suffering from its tyranny."

55. Long and arduous was the journey
to the shore of the ocean of the soul.
"You are the wayfarer's final destiny.
My soul is a drop,
grant me this and I will die and disappear in your expanse."

The ocean replied,
"O' seeker, confused and worn,
from the particle to the galaxy a hundred worlds you sought after me,
but that which is within you, you seldom ponder or want to see.
That which you have lost, if you ever did,
sits within you and your self covers it.
Now that you have reached this far
be sincere, drawn in this ocean and become one with it,
and drown yet again every moment.
And in this wonder,
the more you drown the thirstier you get."

56. "Destiny has decreed that I be in love with You.
Why then this denial, this rejection and distance?
To show You that this is a lover's plea
and not a child's play,
I will utter a burning sigh
and vanish into it," declared the seeker.

57. Once the seeker had waded in the ocean
and become the undoubting soul,
she found both worlds inferior to her essence.
The seeker now pondered all his pain, trials and tears,
all he had surrendered in happiness and sorrows.
"Was it my search?" he thought.
"Ney, it was the Beloved's pull
that in my heart started the quest."
Confounded he now collapsed
and of himself he was erased.

58. "O' my Love, the Soul of all souls,
since there is no one but You in all the worlds,
why this running in circles, this confusion, this search?"
said the seeker drowning in the ocean of souls
and heard:
"So you would appreciate Me even slightly.
For if a gift is just handed to one,
lack of appreciation will bring him down;
but what a treasure's true worth might be
only one who has paid a price stands to realize."

59. It is our soul's love
that keeps our heart alive.
Whatever her Adorable One hands out
in heartless sport or utter coquetry,
be it in our eyes sacrilege or pure blasphemy,
it suits the soul just right and brings her only delight.

ENDNOTES

Abbreviations

AN Kadkani, Dr. M.R. Sh., editor. *Asrar-Nameh* [*The Book of Mysteries*] by Sheikh Farideddin Attar Neyshaboori. From the Attar Collection, no. 4. 1st edition. Tehran, Iran : Sokhan Publications, 2007.

EN Kadkani, Dr. M.R. Sh., editor. *Elahee-nameh* [*The Book of the Beloved*] by Sheikh Farideddin Attar Neyshaboori. From the Attar Collection, no. 2. Tehran, Iran : Sokhan Publications, 2006.

MKN Kadkani, Dr. M.R. Sh., editor. *Mokhtar-nameh* [*The Book of the Sovereign, Attar's Rubais*], by Sheikh Farideddin Attar Neyshaboori, 2nd edition. Tehran, Iran : Sokhan Publications, 1996.

MN Kadkani, Dr. M.R. Sh., editor. *Moseebat-nameh* (*The Book of Travails)* by Sheikh Farideddin Attar Neyshaboori. 1st edition. From the Attar Collection, no. 3. Tehran, Iran: Sokhan Publications, 2007.

DIV Mansour, Jahangeer, editor. *Divan of Attar* by Sheikh Farideddin Attar Neyshaboori. (includes Attar biography by Badiozaman Forozanfar). 5th edition. Tehran, Iran: Negah Publications, Sokhan Publications, 2005.

Frontmatter

1. DIV p. 123, no. 28
2. DIV p. 570, no. 751
3. Prabhavananda, *Upanishads, The Breath of the Eternal*, pp. 27/28
4. Rumi, *Divan of Shams*, p. 342, no. 841

The Poems of Attar

1 EN pp. 111, 112; nos. 1, 25
2 DIV p. 122, no. 28
3 DIV p. 157, no. 34
4 DIV p. 147, no. 18, select
5 DIV p. 195, no. 100
6 DIV p. 584, no. 776
7 EN p. 114, nos. 83-85
8 MN p. 447-448, nos.7105-7120, select
9 EN p. 231
10 EN p. 370, nos. 5706-5710
11 DIV p. 493
12 AN p. 157, nos. 1590-1591
13 MN p. 464, no. 37
14 MN p. 349, nos. 4972-4980
15 MN p. 197, nos. 1730-1734; nos. 1748-1751, select
16 MN p. 465 no. 49
17 MN p. 464 no. 23 - A
18 DIV p.639, no. 18
19 MKN p. 100, no. 202
20 EN p. 32
21 EN p. 259, nos. 2302-2304
22 MKN p. 95, no. 135
23 EN p. 116, nos. 127-128
24 DIV p. 441, no. 508
25 MKN p. 354, no. 2135
26 MN p. 439, no. 6913
27 MN p. 466, no. 87
28 MN p. 238, nos. 2626-2631
29 AN p. 143, nos. 1280-1282
30 AN p. 466, no. 66
31 MKN p. 96, no. 167
32 AN p. 131, no. 1022-1024
33 EN p.307, no. 4336-4338
34 MN p. 332, no. 4600
35 MN p. 937, nos. 2595-2601
36 MN p. 439, nos. 6914-6918
37 EN p. 351, nos. 5298-5305
38 MN p. 277, nos. 2451-2459
39 AN p. 206, nos. 2684-2686
39.1 EN p. 320, nos.4629 - 4632
40 MN p. 237, nos. 2592-2594
41 AN p. 197, nos. 2494-2514
42 MN p. 466, no. 69
43 AN p. 214, nos. 2847-2850
44 MN p. 466, no. 84
45 MN p. 465, no. 55
46 MN p. 193, nos. 1654-1659
47 EN p. 350, nos. 5287-5991
48 AN p. 186, nos. 2235-2237
49 MN p. 191, nos. 1608-1611
50 AN p. 202, nos. 2605-2608
51 MN p. 236, nos. 2564-2571
52 DIV p. 618, no. 834
53 AN p.137, nos. 1160-1161
54 AN p. 138, no. 1167
55 MN p. 192, nos. 1642-1649
56 AN p. 149, nos. 11415-11416
57 DIV p. 427, no. 485
58 AN p. 155, nos. 1548-1551
59 AN p. 144, nos. 1308-1310
60 DIV p. 580, no. 770
61 MN p. 464, no. 17 A
62 MKN p. 93, no. 138
63 EN p. 30
64 AN p. 159, nos. 1640-1641
65 MN p. 359, no. 5180
66 EN p. 117, nos. 141-151, select
67 MN p. 359, nos. 5139-5145
68 MN p. 465, no. 50
69 AN p. 201, nos. 2584-2588
70 DIV p. 464, no. 19 A
71 MN pp. 261-262, nos. 3112-3118
72 MN p. 272, no. 3339-3340
73 DIV p. 238, no. 175
74 DIV p. 334, no. 333
75 DIV p. 417, no. 469
76 DIV p. 627, no. 857
77 DIV p. 488, no. 594
78 MKN p.98, no. 185
79 MN p. 440, nos. 6933-6934
80 MN p. 464, no. 24
81 MN p. 316, no. 4283-4285
82 EN p. 84
83 MN p. 467, no. 99

84 DIV p. 200, no. 106
85 DIV p. 130, no. 30
86 MN p. 452, nos. 7220-7222
87 MKN p. 112, no. 299
88 MN p. 463, no. 7
89 MKN p. 149, no. 578
90 AN p. 159, no. 1630-1632
91 MN p. 443, nos. 6998-7002
92 AN p. 227, no. 3164
93 MN p. 169, nos. 1143-1155, select
94 EN p. 404, no. 6499-6504
95 MN p. 358, no. 5176-5183
96 MN p. 232, no. 2482-2494
97 MN p. 463, no. 8
98 EN p. 333, no. 4908
99 MN p. 466, no. 74
100 MN p. 185, nos. 1502-1508
101 MKN p. 253, no. 2130
102 MN p. 464, no. 75
103 AN p. 212, nos. 2814-2816
104 EN p. 339, nos. 5039-5044
105 MN p. 464, no. 18
106 EN p. 341, no. 5075
107 AN p. 221, no. 3010
108 MN p. 466, no. 64
109 MN p. 405-406, lines 6181-6225
110 DIV p. 308, no. 289
110.1 MN p. 238, nos. 2610-2613
111 MN p. 272, nos. 3846-3352
112 MN p. 401, nos. 6110-6131, select
113 MKN p. 258, no. 2169
114 MN p. 239, no. 2632-2640
115 MKN p. 191, no. 889
116 DIV p. 542, no. 695
117 DIV p. 382, no. 408
118 MN p. 169, nos. 1136-1140
119 EN p. 113, no. 49
120 DIV p. 416, no. 468
121 MN p. 465, no. 47
122 DIV p. 236, no. 172
123 MN p. 465, no. 60
124 MN p. 465, no. 54
125 EN p. 400, no. 6408
126 EN p. 364, nos. 6286-6289
127 MKN p. 85, no. 92
128 EN p. 33
129 MKN p. 359, no. 2174
130 DIV p. 344, no. 350
131 DIV p. 424, no. 482
132 EN p. 307, nos. 4338-4340
133 EN p. 403, nos. 6479-6483
134 AN p. 144, nos. 1298-1304
135 DIV p. 237, no. 174
136 MN p. 452, nos. 7215-7217
137 MN p. 423-426, no. 6555-6631, select
137.1 MN p. 332, nos. 4603-4609
138 AN p. 226, nos. 3138-3140
139 DIV p. 492, no. 602-1
140 MKN p. 98, no. 183
141 AN p. 153, nos. 1507-1581
142 DIV p. 299, no. 275
143 DIV p. 504, no. 624
144 AN p. 217, nos. 2915-2920
145 MN p. 466, no. 79
146 MN p. 467, no. 101
147 MKN p. 166, no. 702
148 DIV p. 451, no. 527
149 MN p. 467, no. 93
150 MKN p. 360, no. 2182
151 DIV p. 576, no. 761
152 MN p. 464, no. 32
153 MN p. 198, nos. 1771-1783
154 MN p. 465, no. 52
155 MN p. 465, no. 38
156 EN p. 406, nos. 6540-6554
157 DIV p. 284, no. 254
158 MN p. 465, no. 62
159 AN p. 216, no. 2898-2908
160 MN p. 464, no. 20
161 MKN p. 175, no. 769
162 AN p. 190, nos. 2322-2328
163 AN p. 175, nos. 1986-1996
164 EN p. 280, no. 3746
165 DIV p. 614, no. 829
166 DIV p. 301, no. 278
167 MN p. 204, nos. 1897-1904, select
168 MN p. 464, no. 31
169 MKN p. 360, no. 2181
170 MKN p. 189, no. 870

171 DIV p. 583, no. 774
172 DIV p. 235, no. 171
173 MKN p. 94, no.152
174 EN p. 365, no. 5604
175 MKN p. 190, no. 880
176 DIV p. 280. no. 246, select
177 MN p. 430, nos. 6722-6727
178 DIV p. 430, no.489
179 Kashkool, p. 82
180 DIV p. 292, no. 261, select
181 MN p. 364, nos. 5300-5302
182 DIV p. 467, no. 96
183 MN p. 382, nos. 5686-5687
184 DIV p. 225-226, no. 154
185 DIV p. 290, no. 259
186 MN p. 249, no. 2830-2833
187 DIV p. 617, no. 833
188 MN p. 237, nos. 2586-2591
189 MN p. 232, nos. 2498-2513, select
190 MN p. 194-195, nos. 1688-1697, select
191 MN p. 453, nos. 7239-7242
192 EN p. 115, no. 100-113
193 MN p. 463, no. 1
194 DIV p. 570, no. 750
195 DIV p. 607, no. 814
196 DIV p. 528, no. 670
197 DIV p. 507, no. 630
198 DIV p. 569, no. 747, select
199 DIV p. 386, no. 414
200 MKN p. 227, no. 1170
201 DIV p. 183, no. 80
202 DIV p.180, no. 74
203 MN p. 431, no.6743
203 MN p. 435, no. 6841
204 EN p. 245, no. 2985-2989
205 MN p. 427, no. 6640-6643
206 EN p. 113, no. 47-48
207 MN p. 388, nos. 5818-5837, select
208 MN p. 431, nos. 6728-6739
209 MN p. 464, no. 25
210 MN p. 464, no. 26
211 AN p. 171, nos. 1898-1890
212 DIV p. 569, no. 747
213 MN p. 465, no. 45
214 AN p. 222, no. 3038
215 MN p. 465, no. 44
216 DIV p. 616, no. 832
217 DIV p. 613, no. 827
218 MN p. 464, no. 14
219 DIV p. 611, no. 821
220 MN p. 464, no. 16
221 DIV p. 517, no. 649
222 MKN p. 225, no. 1393
223 DIV p. 555, no. 721, select
224 MKN p. 222, no. 1132
225 MN p. 463, no. 11
226 MKN p. 141, no. 521
227 MKN p. 107, no. 254
228 MKN p. 100, no. 201
229 MKN p. 162, no. 675
230 MKN p. 99, no. 191
231 MKN p. 102, no. 219
232 MKN p. 215, no. 1083
233 DIV p. 229, no. 160
234 MKN p. 360, no. 2184
235 DIV p. 302, no. 279
236 DIV p. 330, no. 327
237 DIV p. 492, no. 602
238 DIV p. 575, no. 759
239 DIV p. 600, no. 804
240 DIV p. 491, no. 600
241 AN p. 153, nos. 1517-1520
242 MKN p. 112, no. 296
243 MKN p. 104, no. 227
244 DIV p. 206-207, no. 119
245 DIV p. 340, no. 343
246 MKN p. 108, no. 263
247 MKN p. 106, no. 241
248 DIV p. 428, no. 487, select
249 MN p. 81, no. 57
250 AN p. 236, no. 155
251 DIV p. 570, no. 751, line 7
252 DIV p. 143, no. 11
253 EN p. 423, no. 207-218
254 MN p. 465, no. 39
255 MN p. 291, no. 3760-3765
256 AN p. 156, no. 1578-1581
257 AN p. 170, nos.1892-1894
258 AN p. 199, nos. 2527-2528

259 AN p. 149, no. 1428
260 DIV p. 401, no. 440
261 DIV p. 348, no. 357, select
262 DIV p. 515, no. 646
263 DIV p. 483, no. 584
264 DIV p. 424, 434, nos. 483, 496
265 DIV p. 344, no. 349
266 DIV p. 320, no. 309
267 MKN p. 367, no. 2235
268 MKN p. 368, no. 2241
269 MKN p. 130, no. 1811
270 MKN p. 254, no. 1389
271 MKN p. 100, no. 207
272 MKN p. 97, no. 180
273 MKN p. 92, no. 130
274 MKN p. 92, no. 134
275 DIV p. 33
276 MKN p. 351, no. 2116
277 MKN p. 78, no. 29
278 MKN p. 365, no. 2225
279 DIV p. 574, no. 757
280 DIV p. 559, no. 728
281 DIV p. 504, no. 626
282 MKN p. 79, no. 34
283 DIV p. 487, no. 591
284 DIV p. 477, no. 573
285 DIV p. 446, no. 516
286 DIV p. 218-219, nos. 140-141
287 DIV p. 202-203, no. 111
288 DIV p. 443, no. 511
289 DIV p. 532, no. 676
290 DIV p. 161, no. 41
291 MKN p. 352, no. 2133
292 MKN p. 248, no. 1336
293 MKN p. 237, no. 1250
294 MKN p. 151, no. 598
295 MKN p. 234, no. 1230
296 MKN p. 80, no. 50
297 MKN p. 80, no. 48
298 MN p. 463, no. 5
299 MKN p. 80, no. 44
300 MN p. 445, nos. 7062-7066
301 EN p. 412, nos. 6692-6614
302 EN p. 276, no. 3674
303 DIV p. 311, no. 295
304 DIV p. 436, no. 499
305 DIV p. 298, no. 273
306 DIV p. 420, no. 476
307 DIV p. 216, no. 135
308 MKN p. 146, no. 559
309 MKN p. 214, no. 1074
310 MKN p. 107, no. 255
311 MKN p. 364, no. 2217
312 MKN p. 105, no. 239
313 DIV p. 462, no. 9
314 EN p. 395, nos. 6292-6297
315 EN p. 296, nos. 4091-4094
316 AN p. 226, no. 3175
317 MN p. 445, nos. 7046-7047
318 MN p. 463, no. 4
319 MN p. 464, no. 28
320 MN p. 463, no. 6
321 MN p. 443, nos. 7003-7015
322 MN p. 363, nos. 5276-5280
323 DIV p. 468, no. 67
324 MN p. 439, nos. 6920-6922
325 MN p. 233, nos. 2514-2517
326 MKN p. 109, no. 274
327 MN p. 463, no. 10
328 MKN p. 318, no. 1874
329 MKN p. 110, no. 281
330 MKN p. 337, no. 2032
331 MKN p. 372, no. 2275
332 MKN p. 109, no. 268
333 MKN p. 104, no. 229
334 MN p. 439, nos. 6923-6925
335 MKN p. 99, no. 199
336 MKN p. 99, no. 191
337 MN p. 465, no. 43
338 MKN p. 338, no. 2037
339 MKN p. 93, no. 145
340 MKN p. 95, no. 163
341 DIV p. 640, no. 19
342 DIV p. 310, no. 294
343 MN p. 450, nos. 7173-7174
344 DIV p. 217-218, no. 108
345 MN p. 467, no. 102
346 MN p. 446, nos. 7072-7086, select
347 DIV p. 130, no. 29
348 DIV p. 435, no. 498
349 EN p. 403, nos. 6479-6483, select
350 AN p. 232, no. 3265-3272, select

BIBLIOGRAPHY

All titles in Farsi (Persian) have been transliterated into English by Vraje Abramian.

Abedi, Dr. Mahmood, editor. *Nafahat-al Uns* by Nooreddin Abdorrahman Jami. Modern Edition. 5th edition. Tehran, Iran: Sokhan Publications, 2007.

Abramian, Vraje, translator. *Nobody Son of Nobody. Poems of Sheikh Abu-Saeed Abil-Kheir*. Prescott, Arizona: Hohm Press, 2001.

________*The Soul and a Loaf of Bread. The Teachings of Sheikh Abol-Hasan of Kharaqan*. Prescott, Arizona: Hohm Press, 2010.

Aflaki, Shamseddin Ahmad. *Manaqhib-al Arefeen*. Edited and with an introduction by Farsheed Eqbal. 1st edition. Tehran, Iran: Eqbal Publications, 2007.

Ahmadi, Babak. *Four Studies of Tazkarat-ol Olya*. [*Biography of the Saints.*] First Issue. Tehran, Iran: Nashr-e Markaz Publishing Company, P.O. Box 14155-5541, 1998, p. 154.

Ansari, Khaje Abdollah. *Kashf-al Asrar*. (10 vols.) Abridged Farsi version, *Tafseer-e Adabi va Erfany-e Qora'n-e Majid* [*Literary and Mystic Interpretation of the Holy Qor'an*]. Emam Ahmad Meybodi, (2 volumes), 17th edition. Edited by Habibollah Amoozgar. Tehran, Iran: Eqbal Publications, 2004.

Austin, R.W.J., translator. *Ibn-Al-Arabi: The Bezels of Wisdom*. The Classics of Western Spirituality. Preface by Titus Burhardt. N.Y., Toronto, Canada: Paulist Press, 1980.

Baker, Robert and Henry Gray, editors. *Merton and Sufism, the Untold Story, a Complete Compendium*. Kentucky: Fons Vitae, 1999.

Corbin, Henry. *Alone with the Alone. Creative Imagination in the Sufism of Ibn Arabi*. p. 135. 6th edition. Bollingen; Princeton University Press, 1998.

Danner, Victor and Wheeler M. Thackston, editors. *Ibn-Ata-Illah: The Book of Wisdom / Khaja Abdollah Ansari: Intimate Conversations*. The Classics of Western Spirituality. Preface by Annemarie Schimmel. N.Y., Toronto, Canada: Paulist Press, 1978.

Estelami, Dr. Mohammad, editor. "Sheikh Farideddin Attar Neyshaboori" in *Tazkarat-al Oliya (Biography of the Saints)*. 8th edition. Zavvar Publications, 1994.

Heydarkhani, Hosein (Moshtaq-Ali), editor. *Fihi Ma Fihi* (Persian), *In It Is What's In It*, Meeras-e Derakhshan-e Molana Jalaeddin Mohammad Molavi Series, 3rd edition. Tehran, Iran: Sanai Publications, 2002. Farsi.

Kadkani, Dr. M.R. Sh., editor. *Asrar-Nameh* (AN) [*The Book of Mysteries*] by Sheikh Farideddin Attar Neyshaboori. From the Attar Collection, no. 4. 1st edition. Tehran, Iran: Sokhan Publications, 2007.

________. *Elahee-nameh* (EN) [*The Book of the Beloved*] by Sheikh Farideddin Attar Neyshaboori. From the Attar Collection, no. 2. Tehran, Iran : Sokhan Publications, 2006.

________. *Mokhtar-nameh* [*The Book of the Sovereign, Attar's Rubais*], by Sheikh Farideddin Attar Neyshaboori, 2nd edition. Tehran, Iran: Sokhan Publications, 1996.

________. *Moseebat-nameh* (MN) (*The Book of Travails*) by Sheikh Farideddin Attar Neyshaboori. 1st edition. From the Attar Collection, no. 3. Tehran, Iran: Sokhan Publications, 2007.

________. *Neveshte-bar-darya, az miras-e erfani-e Sheikh Abol Hasan-e Kharaqani* [*Scripture on the Sea, from Spiritual Legacy of Sheikh Abol Hasan of Kharaqan.*] Tehran, Iran: Sokhan Publications, 1988. From Original Farsi.

Kadkani, Dr. M. R. Sh. "On the Translatability of Poetry" in *Bukhara Literary Magazine, A Persian Review of Culture, Art and Iranology.* Vol. 14, No. 80, March-April, 2010. Tehran, Iran, pp. 82-88.

Kaseb, Azizollah. editor. *Kashkool-e Sheikh Bahai* (by Bahaoddin Mohammad Abdol-Samad Amoli, known as Sheikh Bahai, d 1606AD/984AH), 9th edition, Goli Publications, Tehran, 2007 (1385).

Lewison, L. *Classical Persian Sufism from its Origins to Rumi.* Foreword by Dr. Javad Nurbakhsh. Great Britain: Introduction by S.H. Nasr. KNP, 1993.

Maktoobat va Majales-e Sabaea. *Letters and Sermons by His Holiness Molana Jalaeddhin (Rumi) Mahammad Balkhi.* Foreword by Dr. Javad Salmasi-Zadeh. 3rd edition. Tehran, Iran: Eqbal Publications, 2005. Farsi.

Mansour, Jahangeer, editor. *Divan of Attar* (DIV) by Sheikh Farideddin Attar Neyshaboori (includes Attar biography by Badiozaman Forozanfar). 5th edition. Tehran, Iran: Negah Publications, 2005.

Masoomi, Reza. *Arefaneha, Jami az Oqianoos-e Beekaran-e Erfan* [*Selections of Mystic Poetry, a Cup from the Infinite Ocean of Gnosi*], 6th edition. Tehran, Iran: Nashre-Eshare Publications, 1991. From original Farsi.

Minavi, Dr. Mojtaba. "The Role of Language and Literature in National Identity" in *Bukhara Literary Magazine, A Persian Review of Culture, Art and Iranology.* Vol. 14, No. 80, March-April, 2010. Tehran, Iran, pp. 521-523.

Pournamdarian, Taqi. *The Vision of Simorqh: Attar's Poetry, Mysticism and Thoughts.* Tehran, Iran: Institute for Humanities and Cultural Studies, 2007.

Prabhavananda, Swami and Frederick Manchester. *Upanishads, the Breath of the Eternal.* Hollywood, Calif.: Vedanta Press, 1983.

Razi, Dr. Hashem. *Hekmat-e Khosravani.* [*The Royal Wisdom from Zoroaster to Sohravardi*]. Tehran, Iran: Behjat Publications, 1979.

Rumi, Jalaleddin. *Kolleeyat-e Shams Tabrizi* [*The Divan of Shams of Tabriz*] from No. 1 to 3365, pages 49 to 1249. With a biography and introduction by Badeeozzaman Foroozanfar. 11th edition. Tehran, Iran: Sepehr Publications, 1998.

Shulte, Rainer and John Biguenet, editors. *Theories of Translation, An Anthology of Essays from Dryden to Derrida.* Chicago, Illinois: The University of Chicago Press, 1992.

Sufism, an Inquiry, Vol. XV, No. 2. San Rafael, Calif.: International Association of Sufism Publications.

Thackston, W.M., Jr., translator. *Signs of the Unseen, The Discourses of Jalauddin Rumi.* Vermont: Threshold Sufi Classics, Threshold Publications, 1994.

ABOUT THE AUTHOR

The poet's original name was Abu-Hamed Mohammad-ebne Ibrahim. He used Attar (shortened from his full religious name, Farideddin Attar Neyshaboori) as his pen name. He was born in 1119 in Kadkan, Khorasan (Iran). He married and had children, but details about his life are sketchy, although his poetic legacy has made him a household name in Persian-speaking homes. Untold seekers on the Path for generations—including other great Sufi mystic poets, like Rumi, who succeeded him—have been nourished by his extensive works. Attar was killed during the Mongol invasion of Khorasan in 1221.

ABOUT THE TRANSLATOR

Vraje Abramian is the translator of three other books published by Hohm Press: *Nobody, Son of Nobody*, *This Heavenly Wine*, and *The Soul and a Loaf of Bread.*

ABOUT HOHM PRESS

Hohm Press is committed to publishing books that provide readers with alternatives to the materialistic values of the current culture, and promote self-awareness, the recognition of interdependence, and compassion. Our subject areas include parenting, transpersonal psychology, religious studies, women's studies, the arts and poetry.

Contact Information: Hohm Press, PO Box 4410, Chino Valley, Arizona, 86323; USA; 800-381-2700, or 928-636-3331; email: hppublisher@cableone.net

Visit our website at www.hohmpress.com